Games, Ideas and Activities
for Primary Mathematics

Other titles in the series

Games, Ideas and Activities for
Primary
Mathematics

John Dabell

Longman
is an imprint of

Harlow, England • London • New York • Boston • San Francisco • Toronto
Sydney • Tokyo • Singapore • Hong Kong • Seoul • Taipei • New Delhi
Cape Town • Madrid • Mexico City • Amsterdam • Munich • Paris • Milan

This book is dedicated to Mr. Iain McVicar and his team at the Queen's Medical Centre in Nottingham for saving my life.

PEARSON EDUCATION LIMITED

Edinburgh Gate
Harlow CM20 2JE
United Kingdom
Tel: +44 (0)1279 623623
Fax: +44 (0)1279 431059
Website: www.pearsoned.co.uk

First edition published in Great Britain in 2009

ISBN: 978-1-4082-2320-8

British Library Cataloguing in Publication Data
A CIP catalogue record for this book can be obtained from the British Library

Library of Congress Cataloging in Publication Data
A CIP catalog record for this book can be obtained from the Library of Congress

10 9 8 7 6 5 4 3 2
13 12 11 10

Set by 30
Printed by Ashford Colour Press, Gosport

Contents

Introduction

Purpose

This book contains a collection of games and activities for use in the maths classroom and provides opportunities for children to develop as learners in a wide variety of ways. They have all been tried and tested in my own classrooms over the years and shared with colleagues in KS1 and KS2. The activities are designed to introduce and reinforce mathematical concepts and can provide a rich source of ideas for achieving and consolidating many curricular objectives.

At the heart of all the activities is active participation and collaborative learning. Each activity will help children improve their speaking and listening skills by interpreting, discussing, following rules, making decisions and asking questions. Playing the games and activities in this book will also help children to

- use and extend their mathematical vocabulary
- explore, express, discuss and argue mathematical ideas
- think and work mathematically
- build mathematical confidence
- improve their concentration
- develop positive attitudes towards maths
- learn the value of talking mathematically and working together to achieve understanding
- experience maths in a thought-provoking and exciting environment
- cultivate mathematical development by building and extending current knowledge and understanding
- freely explore a range of concepts, reinforcing and extending their skills.

Practical, hands-on and minds-on maths activities such as those contained in this resource will, over a relatively short space of time, help children to

- improve the efficiency of their mental calculations and extend informal pencil-and-paper procedures
- think creatively and have fun doing maths
- work cooperatively and support each other
- compete sensibly and play fair
- record thinking in a variety of ways
- devise new ways of working

- discuss different strategies and approaches
- use logic and reasoning
- become junior problem-solvers
- prove or disprove a rule
- simplify or complicate a game or puzzle
- adapt games and invent their own.

Games and activities help children get a much better feel for what maths is all about, what it can do and how it does it. Games and activities help teachers see children in new contexts. They can help teachers get to grips with the levels of sophistication children are working at, talk through inconsistencies and respond to challenges. They help to inform assessment because pupils reveal what they know, what they don't know and what they partly know. This makes next steps in learning more diagnostic and suited to the needs of learners.

Sometimes, it is said that when children are involved in games they don't really realise they are doing maths. That is not the intention of this book. We want children to recognise the maths they are using and make use of it in other situations. It is down to us to make the maths explicit if it isn't already obvious to children and to further exploit maths opportunities whenever they arise.

How to use this book

The games and activities can be used at the beginning of a lesson, as a main lesson focus, as part of a guided maths session or within the plenary. They could also be used outside a maths lesson. To get the most out of the activities, it is important to be clear about why you are using them. If you plan to use them just for fun then they could form a part of your reward system for completing work, used in a maths golden time or within a maths club. If your aim is to practise a key skill or process then you will use the activities more strategically as part of your planning linked to the concept you are pinpointing. Some games might be taken home as part of the homework policy too. You might use a game or activity as part of a display to stimulate discussion.

However you decide to use the book, each activity needs careful explanation so that children know what to do, although try to avoid long-winded instructions, as children will be keen to get started. It is hoped that the games and activities will be used regularly rather than just now and again. Although you and your class might have a favourite, it is important to introduce new games in order to build new skills.

The games and activities have been designed to be as practical as possible using resources readily available in the classroom. You may, however, have to make specific provisions for children with special needs, e.g. enlarging text.

Many of the games are key stage specific, but they can be easily adapted to suit the needs of your learners. If you look at an activity and think it might not have a low enough access point, then it might require only a small modification to make it usable. When trying out the games and activities it is worth bearing in mind that you will find some that work really well with your class, some that work reasonably well whilst others might just fall flat. There is no such thing as a universally challenging activity where one size fits all. It is worth building up a file of all the games, activities and investigations that you use and annotating them with how they worked, any problems that arose and what you would do differently next time. The success of the games and activities will largely be down to the teacher and the extent to which dialogue and discussion are encouraged. Where possible, move between pairs/groups, listen for a while, intervene strategically and engage them by asking probing questions, provoking discussion and responding to answers (see appendices for types of thinking questions you could use).

Children need to be challenged by activities that encourage them to think and talk about their ideas and it is hoped that this resource will play a part in establishing games and activities as a normal part of daily maths work stimulating junior maths brains.

You will find some useful items in the appendices: there are some thinking questions you could use; multiplication and division facts; factors of numbers 1–100; prime numbers less than 100; composite numbers less than 100; square numbers 1–400; The four-step problem-solving process; and a glossary of maths terms.

Page layout

Each activity comes with a brief description to give you a flavour of what the activity is about. The 'Learning objectives' are linked to the National Curriculum programmes of study and the New Framework. A 'Resources' section tells you what equipment you will need for the activity. In some cases, a worksheet will be referred to which links to our dedicated website. These will bring games to life and make them exciting to use. 'What to do' describes the instructions for games or what steps you might choose to take within an activity. 'Variations' offers you some ideas for making tweaks and changes to the activity to adapt it in some way. 'Challenge questions' provide food for thought extensions to test you further.

Acknowledgements

Two beautiful people have helped support me writing this book, my wife Wendy and my daughter Maisy. Thank you both for everything.

I also want to thank the children and teachers of Roe Green Primary School (London), Derby High Junior School (Derby), Lawn Primary School (Derby) and Forest Fields Primary and Nursery (Nottingham).

About the author

John Dabell trained as a primary teacher 15 years ago and his teaching career is now based in Nottingham. During that time he has trained as an Ofsted inspector and has worked as a national inservice provider and writer. John has written 1,000 education articles and is the author of four books and co-author of three other titles. See www.johndabell.co.uk.

Chapter 1
Place value

Number criteria

Number criteria is a great game for ordering three digits from a choice of five to meet different number criteria.

Suitable for

KS2

Aims

- To read and write numbers with three digits.
- Know what each digit represents in terms of its place and face value.

Players

- A game for two players

Resources

- Paper and pencils
- Digit cards 0–9
- Number criteria grid

What to do

- Organise children into pairs and give them each a copy of the Number criteria grid shown here.
- Players shuffle a set of digit cards and deal out five.
- For each round, players look at their five cards and select three to match the criteria. For example, one player may have the following cards 9 7 2 1 8 and another player may have 2 3 7 8 6.
  For round 1 one player could make 987 and the other could make 876 so player 1 would win. There are 3 points for a win.
- The player with the most points at the end of the game is the winner.

Round	Game 1	Points	Game 2	Points
1. Largest number				
2. Smallest number				
3. Largest odd number				
4. Smallest odd number				
5. Largest even number				
6. Smallest even number				
7. Nearest to 500				
8. Furthest away from				

Variations

- You could invent a range of number criteria, such as 'number made up of three prime digits' or ' number closest to a score', etc.
- Include more than 8 rounds.
- Instead of dealing five cards, deal 4 or 6.
- Play the game to 4-digit numbers or reduce to 2-digit numbers.

Challenge questions

- Can you invent a new scoring system?
- What new targets/number criteria can you think of for your own game?

Know your place

Know your place is a clever activity for reading and writing 4-digit numbers.

Suitable for

KS2

Aims

- To read and write numbers with three or more digits.
- Know what each digit represents in terms of its place and face value.

Players

- A game for two players

Resources

- Paper and pencils
- Digit cards 0–9 x 3
- Know your place boards 1 and 2

What to do

- Organise children into pairs and give each child the Know your place boards as shown here.

Know your place board 1

Seven thousand and sixty-nine

—— —— —— ——

One thousand three hundred and one

—— —— —— ——

Five thousand, nine hundred and fourteen

—— —— —— ——

Know your place board 2

Four thousand one hundred and two

____ ____ ____ ____

Nine thousand eight hundred

____ ____ ____ ____

Seven thousand, five hundred and seventy-eight

____ ____ ____ ____

- Shuffle the number cards and place them face down in a pile on the table.
- Players take it in turns to take a card and write the number in one of the empty spaces under the written number.
- If you cannot place a number then the card is returned to the pile.
- The winner is the first player to fill in all the empty spaces.

Variations

- You can increase the number of digits to a 5- or 6-digit number.
- Players can use the same board and write the numbers they place in a different colour. The player with the most numbers in their colour wins.
- Play the game but reverse the numbers to make new numbers, e.g. 3672 would become 2763.

Challenge questions

- Discuss how fair the game would be to include a number with four digits that are the same. Could that person win?
- Can you invent a decimal version of this game?

Bullseye

> Bullseye is a place value target activity that helps children approximate to the nearest 10.

Suitable for

KS1
KS2

Aims

- To approximate to the nearest 10.
- Know what each digit represents in terms of its place and face value.

Players

- A game for two or more players

Resources

- Paper and pencils
- Digit cards 0–9
- Bullseye grid

What to do

- Organise children into pairs and give each player copies of the Bullseye grid as on page 7.
- Shuffle the cards and put them in a pile face down on the table.
- Player A takes one card and places it in any empty square next to a target number.
- Player B takes a card and does the same.
- Players take it in turns taking cards and placing them in empty boxes.

Target number	Number made		Points scored
10	1	2	15
20	2	0	20
30	3	4	0
40			
50			
60			
70			
80			
90			

- Points are scored as follows:
  20 points for hitting the target and making the number exactly.
  15 points for making a number two away, e.g. if the target number
  was 10 and someone made either 08 or 12 then 15 points would be
  scored.
- The winner is the player who has the most points after all the boxes
  have been filled with digits.

Variations

- You can play this game for numbers other than multiples of 10.
- Instead of placing a digit anywhere, start at 10 and work your way through to
  90, so whatever digit you pick up has to go in one of the boxes next to the
  target number of 10.
- Change the rules so that points are scored for getting within 5 of a target
  number.
- Progress on to target numbers over 100.
- Try this game for decimal numbers too.

Challenge questions

- What does each digit represent in terms of its face and place value?
- How many odd/even numbers did you make?
- Can you find out the digital root for each of the numbers you made?

Bish, bash, bosh

Bish, bash, bosh is an enjoyable activity that helps children get to grips with identifying numbers, place and face value.

Suitable for

KS1
KS2

Aims

- Read and write whole numbers from 0 to 99.
- Know what each digit represents in terms of its place and face value.

Players

- A game for two players

Resources

- Paper and pencils
- Digit cards 0–9
- Bish, bash, bosh guessing grid

What to do

- Organise children into pairs and give out copies of the Bish, bash, bosh guessing grid.
- One player picks two digit cards and makes a 2-digit number. The cards are turned over face down on the table.
- Player two tries to guess the number written down using the guessing grid.
- The first player ticks in the correct column according to whether the number guessed is a bish, a bash or a bosh. For example, the bish column means that the guesser has one correct digit but in the wrong position. The bash column means the guesser has one correct digit in the correct position. The bosh column means that the guesser has nothing correct.

- The second player continues guessing until the correct number is guessed.
- Players swap over and play the game again using a different guessing grid.

Guess	BISH Correct digit, wrong position	BASH Correct digit, right position	BOSH Nothing correct
1			
2			
3			
4			
5			
6			
7			
8			
9			
10			
11			
12			
13			
14			
15			

Variations

- You can play this game using two sets of digit cards to make a 3-digit number.
- If the player who is guessing hasn't guessed their number after 12 attempts then they lose their go.
- Points can be scored according to how quickly a number is guessed. For example, first guess correct = 100 points, 2–5 guesses = 30 points, 6–10 guesses = 15 points and so on.

Challenge questions

- What does each digit represent in terms of its face and place value?
- Can you find the digital root of each number you guess?

Number of the lesson

Number of the lesson is a great activity that hones and improves children's knowledge and understanding of a variety of number properties.

Suitable for

KS1
KS2

Aims

- To know what factors and multiples are.
- To recognise types of number such as prime, composite and square.
- Know what each digit represents in terms of its place and face value.

Players

- This activity is for the whole class but can be played in small groups or pairs.

Resources

- Paper and pencils
- Dice or digit cards 0–9
- Number of the lesson grid

What to do

- Randomly select any number using digit cards or rolling some dice. You can decide whether to focus on a single-digit number or higher but aim for a mixture of numbers through the week.
- Now tell children that you are going to ask them a dozen questions relating to that number which they then have to work out. For example:

Number of the lesson 24

Round the number to the nearest 10	
Write down all of the factors	
Multiply by 10	
Multiply by 100	
Divide by 10	
Divide by 100	
What is the nearest multiple of 9?	
Find 10%	
Find 5%	
Find 15%	
What is $\frac{2}{3}$ of the number?	
What is the nearest square number?	

- Tell the children that they don't have to answer the questions in order. If they get stuck on one they move on to a question they can answer.
- Work through 'Number of the lesson' together to familiarise children with the activity and share answers. Use the session to find out what children know and don't know about number properties in order to plan future questions.
- Select a new number for the plenary and ask children to answer the questions against the clock. For example, complete the grid in under 2 minutes.

Variations

- You can vary the questions depending on what you want to focus on. You can add more questions or just concentrate on a few and theme them if you wish. For example, you may want to ask questions for one week relating to factors, rounding, multiplying by 10 and dividing by 10.
- You could select decimal numbers, fractions or negative numbers. Questions could be tailored accordingly. For example, 'What is 1 less than the number?', 'Is the number greater than or smaller than $\frac{2}{7}$?', etc.
- Provide different table groups with the same number but different questions or different numbers and the same questions.

- Provide children with similar activities for homework.
- At the end of the week, revise the questions covered and assess children's knowledge and understanding through a test.
- Have a head-to-head competition where children compete against each other to complete the number questions in the fastest time.

Challenge questions

- What questions would you ask? Devise a set of questions for another group to answer in relation to the number of the lesson.
- Can you find examples of the number of the lesson around the school or outside of school?
- Can you find out more about the number of the lesson? For example, search some number websites and see what you can discover (e.g. **www.counton.org**)

Take four digits

Take four digits is an excellent activity that tests children's knowledge and understanding of a variety of number properties.

Suitable for

KS1
KS2

Aims

- To know what factors and multiples are.
- To recognise types of number such as prime, composite and square.
- Know what each digit represents in terms of its place and face value.

Players

- This game is best played in pairs or as a whole class

Resources

- Paper and pencils
- Digit cards 1–9

What to do

- Shuffle a pack of 1–9 digit cards.
- Ask one of the children to select four of the cards. Write these numbers on the board, e.g. 9372.
- Now challenge children to use the four digits to answer the following questions:
  a) Find a 2-digit number > than a score
  b) Find a 3-digit number > than a gross
  c) Find a 4-digit number < than 5,000
  d) Which number is a factor of 28?
  e) Which are prime numbers?
  f) Are there any composite numbers?
  g) How many square numbers are there?

h) Can you find two 2-digit numbers with a difference of 66?

i) What is the digital root of the number?

j) What is the product of the two largest numbers?

Variations

- You could select fewer cards or more cards as appropriate.
- Select six 2-digit numbers and ask questions around these. For example, what is the sum of the three largest numbers subtract the smallest number?
- Play the activity against the clock competing in small groups.
- Include additional questions that test addition, subtraction, multiplication and division. For example, add the three smallest digits and multiply by the largest.

Challenge questions

- Of the four numbers you have selected, which is the odd one out and why?
- Can you invent five questions of your own?

Number splat

> Number splat helps children with determining numbers that are greater than, less than or equal to.

Suitable for

KS1
KS2

Aims

- To use the greater than (>) and less than (<) signs.
- To state inequalities using the symbols < and >.
- Know what each digit represents in terms of its place and face value.

Players

- A game for two players

Resources

- Paper and pencils
- Three dice, two 1–6 dice and another die labelled <, <, >, >, =, =
- Coloured counters

What to do

- Organise children into maths buddies and give out a copy of the Number splat grid as follows:
- Player A rolls the dice and covers a number on the Number splat board that matches what is thrown. For example, if a more than sign is thrown with a 2 and a 6 then any number greater than 26 can be 'splatted' or covered.
- If a number has already been covered then another number has to be chosen.

- If a player rolls a number and an equal sign then that number is covered, e.g. a 1 and = would mean 1 is covered.
- The winner is the first player to cover any five numbers in a row, column or diagonal.

1	2	3	4	5	6
7	8	9	10	11	12
13	14	15	16	17	18
19	20	21	22	23	24
25	26	27	28	29	30
31	32	33	34	35	36

Variations

- The number grid could be made smaller.
- The number grid doesn't have to start at 1. You could create a grid starting at 20.
- Use other numbers on a die apart from 1–6.
- Four in a row to win or another combination of your choosing.
- Throw a double and remove a counter of your opponents.
- Play the game until all the numbers are covered. The numbers covered equal the points you score. The winner is the player with the most points.
- Play the game using a die, labelled >,>,> and <,<,< rather than use any equal signs.
- Play with three numbered dice and alter the numbers on the Number splat grid.
- Have a die labelled <,<,<,>,> and a blank face. If the blank face is rolled then miss a go.

Challenge questions

- Would the game be fair if you used just one > sign and five < signs?
- Could you invent a similar game for practising greater than/less than in relation to fractions?
- Rather than a 6 x 6 grid, what other arrangement could you use?

Number roundup

Number roundup is a challenging activity to help children improve their rounding skills.

Suitable for

KS2

Aims

* To round numbers to 10, 100, 1000, 10,000 and 100,000.
* Know what each digit represents in terms of its place and face value.

Players

* This game is best played in pairs or as a whole class

Resources

* Paper and pencils
* Stopwatches (enough for one between two)

What to do

* Write the following number on the board: 573,526.
* Now explain to children that their challenge is to round that number to the nearest 10, 100, 1000, 10,000 and 100,000 in the fastest time possible.
* Set the stopwatch and challenge the class as a whole. After the first person has completed the task, stop the clock and go through the answers. For example,

Nearest 10 = 573,526
Nearest 100 = 573,530
Nearest 1000 = 574,000
Nearest 10 000 = 570,000
Nearest 100 000 = 600,000

- Now set a similar challenge for children to do in pairs using the following numbers: 645,321; 998,456; 676,766; 420,865; 323,323; 101,909; 909,009; 123,456; 111,111; 500,550.
- Score as follows: all numbers accurately rounded in under 15 seconds = 25 points; over 15 seconds = 0 points.

Variations

- Smaller numbers could be used as appropriate.
- Play the activity without a time limit.
- Play in table groups and race against each other.
- Play 'beat the teacher' and challenge children to beat your time.

Challenge questions

- After rounding, can you find the digital root of each number?
- Can you identify the individual digits that make up the number? For example, 123,456; 1 = square, 2 = prime, 3 = prime, etc.

Number hats

Number hats is an activity designed to help children practise ordering a variety of numbers.

Suitable for

KS2

Aims

- To examine and order whole numbers, decimal numbers, fractions and negative numbers.
- Know what each digit represents in terms of its place and face value.

Players

- A game for large groups or the whole class

Resources

- Number hats (cone hats made out of paper) or sticky labels
- Paper and pencils

What to do

- Make some simple number hats and write the following numbers on them:
  99,099; 9.99; 9.09; –99; 909,009; 99.99; –9.9; 909; 99.9; 0.9
- Pass the hats to 10 children and give them 3 minutes to get their hats in order from the smallest to the largest. The rest of the class could try to place the numbers on a number line in small groups.
- When children have ordered themselves, discuss with the rest of the class whether they think the numbers are standing in order.
  Reposition any number hats that might need moving.

- Try the activity again with a different set of numbers of your choosing. For example, you could try –17, –24, 37, 3.75, –50.05, 941, 0.018, $\frac{1}{2}$, 919, –99.

Variations

- You could use fewer hats and focus on just a few numbers to start with.
- Order the numbers from the biggest to the smallest.
- Increase or decrease the time limit and make it a competition between groups.
- Play a guessing game with just one number. Nine hats know their number but one hat doesn't. This person then has to work out their number asking the rest of the class questions such as 'Am I bigger than 1?', etc.

Challenge questions

- If you reverse the digits in your number, where would you need to stand in a number line now? Are you bigger or smaller? What is the difference between your new number and your original number?

The gharial's mouth

> The gharial's mouth is a game for helping children recognise and use the mathematical signs > and <.

Suitable for

KS2

Aims

- To use and apply the signs < and >.
- Know what each digit represents in terms of its place and face value.

Players

- A game for 4 players

Resources

- Paper and pencils (or whiteboard and pen)
- One die

What to do

- Get children to draw boxes separated by < signs as follows. For example,
- Children take it in turns to roll the die once each.
- After each roll players write down the number shown on the die in one of their boxes on their sheet or whiteboard.
- Once a number is placed, it cannot be changed.
- If the number sequence made is correct, then your score is the number on the left. If not, your score is zero.

Variations

- Instead of playing with the < sign, mix the game so that both < and > are practised. Remember to alter how the points are scored according to the direction of the signs.
- You could make this easier by using just 1-digit boxes.
- Complicate the game by adding two more boxes, one for a decimal point and another for one more digit.
- Instead of drawing boxes next to each other, play the game where you draw boxes one above the other to practise greater than and less than fractions.

Challenge questions

- Can you think of an easy way to remember the signs < and >?
- What happens if the numbers you scored on either side of the sign are the same? Is there a sign to symbolise this?

Make a row

Make a row is an excellent game for practising the rounding of decimal numbers to the nearest tenth.

Suitable for

KS2

Aims

- To round a decimal number to its nearest tenth.
- To use and understand place and face value.

Players

- This game is best played in pairs

Resources

- Paper and pencils (or whiteboard and pen)
- Two sets of number cards (0–9)
- Sets of coloured counters
- A decimal number grid

What to do

- Deal three number cards each.
- Combine the three digits to make a decimal number, e.g. 4.56.
- If your number to its nearest tenth matches one of the numbers on the decimal number board then cover it with a counter. See the number grid shown here.
- If the number you have made does not match a number on the number grid then no counter can be placed.
- Continue like this until the first player gets three in a row either vertically, diagonally or horizontally.

7.1	1.8	5.2	7.4
6.5	1.4	8.3	4.9
6.9	4.7	2.5	9.7
8.2	2.7	3.5	6.4
6.3	2.8	2.8	3.8
1.5	9.1	5.7	4.6

Variations

- Play the game again but reverse the decimals, e.g. 7.1 becomes 1.7.
- Increase the decimal number grid in size to include more rows and columns.
- Allow children to select four cards at the beginning, from which they then select three.
- Make a rule that allows a player to place a counter on top of a number already covered by a counter.

Challenge questions

- Can you turn each decimal number into a mixed fraction?
- Can you invent a new rule for the game? For example, the first player to get a counter in each of the four corners is the winner.

Nearest and dearest

> Nearest and dearest is a game to practise using decimal numbers. It enables children to quickly recognise tenths and hundredths.

Suitable for

KS2

Aims

- To recognise decimal numbers.
- Know what each digit represents in terms of its place and face value.

Players

- A game for 2 players

Resources

- Paper and pencils (or whiteboard and pen)
- Rounding activity sheet

What to do

- Give children a copy of the 'Rounding' activity board as shown on page 26.
- Tell children that they have to choose three of the digits at the top of the table in each column to make the nearest numbers. Go through an example or two together first.
- Remind children that each digit can only be used once.
- When children have completed the table, they check their answers with a partner or another group.
- Repeat the activity selecting your own set of four digits.

	9.1.3.2	3.6.2.4	6.7.0.5	2.9.4.8
Nearest to 1	1.23	2.34	0.76	2.48
Nearest to 2				
Nearest to 2.5				
Nearest to 3				
Nearest to 4				
Nearest to 5				
Nearest to 5.5				
Nearest to 6				
Nearest to 7				
Nearest to 8				
Nearest to 9				
Nearest to 9.5				
Nearest to 10				

Variations

- Increase the number of digits in the top box.
- Select the digits in the top box by rolling a 0–5 die twice and a 4–9 die twice.
- Increase the 'Nearest' aspect of this game to a number of your choosing.

Challenge questions

- Can you write the numbers you have made on a number line?
- Can you say and write each number you have made? For example, 1.23 is said as one point two three and not one point twenty-three.

Digit dance

> Digit dance is an activity to help children practise recognising and naming large numbers.

Suitable for

KS2

Aims

- To name and recognise large numbers.
- To add 1, 10, 100, 1,000 and other powers of 10 to a set of numbers.

Players

- A game for 2 players

Resources

- Paper and pencils (or whiteboard and pen)
- Two sets of 0–9 digit cards per pair
- Digit dance number table

What to do

- Give children sets of digit cards and a copy of the digit dance number table as shown below:
- Explain that there are three large numbers at the top of the sheet which have been chosen by selecting digit cards at random.
- Say that they have to fill in the table by adding 1, 10, 100, 1,000, 10,000, 100,000 and 1,000,000 each time.
- How quickly can they complete the table without making a mistake?
- When children have completed their tables, agree on the new totals.
- Now, using the digit cards, draw out seven cards each time to make three new numbers. Do the same adding again.

Number	2.908.621	3.551.962	8.927.009
+1	2,908,622		
+10			
+100			
+1,000			
+10,000			
+100,000			
+1,000,000			

Variations

- Children should read and write the numbers they make in words.
- You can provide 'tricky' numbers as starting points for children such as 999, 1099 and 1,010,101 to assess their place value knowledge and understanding.
- The numbers added each time can be changed to +15, +30, etc.

Challenge questions

- Can you add up the column of numbers when you have completed the table?
- Can you reverse the digits you start with and then add +1, +10, etc. each time?
- Can you recognise each individual digit in the number you have made and say its place and face value?

Big numbers

> Big numbers is an enjoyable and active activity to help children learn and recognise large numbers.

Suitable for

KS2

Aims

- To read and say large whole numbers.
- Know what each digit represents in terms of its place and face value.

Players

- A game for the whole class

Resources

- Sheets of paper with large numbers written on them (see below)

What to do

- Write the following numbers on pieces of paper big enough to be visible in the classroom or hall space.

    333,013
    303,313
    331,003
    300,003,003
    30,333
    3,030,013
    300,030,033

- Stick the numbers on the walls around the class – a hall would be better.

- Explain to children that you are going to read out some numbers which they then have to go and stand next to. You could do this as a whole class or in small groups.

  > Thirty thousand, three hundred and thirty-three
  > Three hundred and three thousand, three hundred and thirteen
  > Three hundred million, thirty thousand and thirty-three
  > Three hundred and thirty-three thousand and thirteen
  > Three million, thirty thousand and thirteen
  > Three hundred and thirty-one thousand and three
  > Three hundred million, three thousand and three

- Anyone not standing next to the correct number is out.
- As the game progresses you can impose a time limit to reach the numbers.

Variations

- Girls race to one number and boys to another number.
- Write additional numbers to replace those practised.
- Write the digits 0 and 3 onto separate pieces of paper for children to hold or stick on their jumpers. Read out the numbers again and get children to physically make the numbers.
- Try playing the game with digits 0–9 and make various numbers other than those made up of just two digits.

Challenge questions

- Can you reverse the large numbers (ignoring the commas or repositioning the commas in some cases) and say them? For example, 3,030,013 would become 3,100,303.
- Can you halve the numbers and say them? For example, 333,013 would become 166, 506.5.

Number roundup

Number roundup is an enjoyable board game for helping children round up 3-digit numbers to the nearest 10 and 100.

Suitable for

KS2

Aims

- Round 3-digit numbers to the nearest 10 or 100 and give estimates for their sums and differences.
- Know what each digit represents in terms of its place and face value.

Players

- A game for two players

Resources

- 3 dice
- A coin
- Different coloured counters

What to do

- Organise children into pairs and give them a copy of the number grid shown here.
- Decide who will go first. Roll the three dice.
- Now write down all the 3-digit numbers you can make with these three numbers. You cannot use a digit twice. For example, if you roll 1, 2 and 3 then you can make 123, 132, 213, 231, 321, 312.
- Now toss a coin. If it lands on heads then round the 3-digit numbers you have made to the nearest 10. If it lands on tails then you round the 3-digit numbers to the nearest 100. For example, if the coin landed on tails then 123 = 100, 132 = 100, 213 = 200, 231 = 200, 321 = 300 and 312 = 300.

- Now place a counter on each square which has a number you made. So in this example, you would put a counter on 100, 200 and 300.
- The winner is the person with the most counters on the board after seven turns each.

200	520	220	320	300	510	600	430	630	200
400	260	200	100	400	110	220	600	400	600
500	300	430	300	520	210	200	340	500	150
350	430	100	420	500	650	120	100	640	170
540	200	370	220	300	460	660	700	230	670
500	440	260	550	130	250	500	600	310	200
400	100	330	620	300	400	300	560	240	450
120	500	360	600	570	160	700	500	630	470
700	200	100	270	430	150	100	660	250	400
600	300	100	310	260	460	640	500	340	410

Variations

- Make the grid smaller such as a 8 x 8 and populate with different numbers.
- Rather than make all the 3-digit numbers you can, make one 3-digit number.
- If you throw a heads, lose your go. If you throw a tails then you can round to the nearest 10 or 100.
- You could adapt this game for rounding to the nearest 1000. Play with four dice and change the numbers inside the board.
- You could play with different numbered dice. For example, you could try 4–9 dice.

Challenge questions

- Can you invent a version of the game with six dice? For example, you throw six dice and discard three to make 3-digit numbers.
- Can you think of another way of selecting whether to round to the nearest 10 and 100 other than tossing a coin? For example, you could throw one die and if you throw a 1, 2 or 3 then round to the nearest 10 and throw a 4, 5 or 6 and round to the nearest 100.
- If you throw three dice, is it possible to make more than six 3-digit numbers?

Round it up

Round it up is a great activity for helping children learn how to round a decimal number correct to one decimal place.

Suitable for

KS2

Aims

- Round decimal numbers to one decimal place.
- Know what each digit represents in terms of its place and face value.

Players

- A game for two players

Resources

- 0–9 digit cards x 2
- Pencil and paper

What to do

- Organise children into pairs and give them each a set of 0–9 digit cards.
- Ask each player to draw the grid shown here.

U	.	t	h	th

- Shuffle the cards and place them on the table face down.
- One player then selects a card and both players then write that number inside one of the empty boxes on their number grid.
- This is repeated three times until both players have filled their grids.

- Players then round their number correct to one decimal place. For example, if the digits selected are 3.469 then this would be rounded up to 3.5 and 5 points would be scored.
- Points are scored according to the face value of the tenths digit.
- Play ten times.
- The winner is the player with the most points at the end of the ten rounds.

Variations

- Points can be scored differently. For example, instead of face value points, points can be equal to their place value and these added together at the end of the game.
- Instead of rounding to one decimal place, round to two decimal places and score according to the decimal part of the number made. For example, if the digits selected are 7.628 then this would be rounded to 7.63 and 63 points scored.

Challenge questions

- Can you play this game where you round to three decimal places?
- Can you invent a new scoring system? For example, what about saying that the first person to make 12 is the winner?

Chapter 2
Addition

Across the road

Across the road is an addition activity for practice in adding single-digit numbers.

Suitable for

KS1

Aim

● Derive and recall all pairs of numbers with a total of 12.

Players

● A game for two players

Resources

● Across the road number pavements
● Coloured counters
● 1–6 dice

What to do

● Children get into pairs.
● Give each player six counters of one colour each.
● Give each pair the Across the road number pavements. The strips are presented on one sheet with a gap between them. Imagine the gap to be a road and the strips as pavements.

1	2	3	4	5	6	7	8	9	10	11	12

12	11	10	9	8	7	6	5	4	3	2	1

● Choose a number strip and place your counters next to any of the numbers. More than one counter can be placed next to a number.

- Now throw two dice and add them together. If the total is equal to a number where you have placed a counter then that counter can cross over the road. Only one counter can move if you have placed more than one on a number.
- The winner is the first person to get all their counters across the road.

Variations

- The numbers on the number pavements could be changed. For example, if you used 4–9 dice then you could use numbers from 8 to 18.
- The player to get four counters across the road could be the winner.
- If you get a counter across the road then you get another go.
- If you get a counter across the road, it turns into the same coloured counter as your opponent and it can be placed next to any number on their number pavement.

Challenge questions

- Can you adapt this game to practise multiplication? For example, could you replace the numbers 1–12 with 1–36?
- How fair would it be to only have 12 numbers in this game? Would you need to make the number pavements longer?

Take a roll

Take a roll is an addition activity for practice in adding decimals with one decimal place.

Suitable for

KS2

Aims

- To add decimal numbers.
- Use standard column procedures to add decimals.

Players

- A game for two players

Resources

- Take a roll number strip
- Number board
- Coloured counters
- 1–6 die

What to do

- Give each pair of players a copy of both resource sheets shown here.

Take a roll number strip

1	2	3	4	5	6
5.6	3.7	3.2	6.2	2.5	4
2	6.8	1.4	4.2	5.3	4.8

Number grid

9.5	7.8	9.4	6.5	6.2	10
9.8	8	7.7	10.8	5.4	9.3
9.5	5.7	9.7	12.4	10.9	8.2
5.6	10.5	4.6	10.4	6.7	7.6

- Take turns to throw the die twice. On the first roll choose a decimal number underneath the number rolled. Do this again on the second roll and add the two numbers together.
- If the answer is on the grid then place a counter on the number.
- The winner is the first player to get three counters in a row.

Variations

- The numbers on the Take a roll number strip can be changed for numbers of your own choice. Combinations of numbers can be added together to generate the numbers for the grid.
- When you place a counter on the grid, say the number and then round up or down to score that many points. Rather than three in a row, players try to cover the grid or play against the clock and the winner with the most points is the winner.
- Play a version of this game to practise subtraction, multiplication or division.

Challenge questions

- Can you invent a similar game for practising decimals with two decimal places?
- Can you play the game where you reverse the numbers on the Take a roll number strip and then add the numbers to make new numbers for the grid?
- Can you invent bonus throws for making certain numbers? For example, if you make a decimal number where the tenth is $\frac{9}{10}$ then have another go.

Alphaworth

Alphaworth is an addition activity that helps children order numbers to 1,000 and know number names.

Suitable for

KS1
KS2

Aims

- To add numbers 1, 5, 10, 20, 50 and 100
- To understand place and face value.

Players

- An activity to be completed independently, in pairs or in small groups

Resources

- Paper and pencils (or whiteboard and pen)
- Alphaworth sheet

What to do

- Give each pair an Alphaworth sheet as on page 41.
- Write the name of a maths shape on the board and ask children to work out how much the shape is worth. For example, CIRCLE would mean $1 + 1 + 10 + 1 + 5 + 5 = 23$.
- Ask children to find out which shape has the biggest value from the following: square, rectangle, triangle, pentagon.
- Discuss the totals made to see if there is agreement.
- Ask children to investigate the totals for their own names. Who in the class has the largest total? The smallest total? Who have totals that are the same?

	Value
A	100
B	20
C	1
D	50
E	5
F	100
G	10
H	10
I	1
J	100
K	50
L	5
M	10
N	100
O	20
P	50
Q	100
R	10
S	50
T	1
U	20
V	10
W	100
X	20
Y	10
Z	1

Variations

- Use this activity to focus on weekly spellings or subject-specific words such as science words.
- Focus on the names of animals and see who has the largest total.
- Use a calculator for those children who experience difficulty.

Challenge questions

- Can you think of ways of assigning different values to the letters of the alphabet? Why not give them a monetary value? You could give the vowels one value and the consonants another, such as vowels are 7p and conso- nants are 3p. Set a puzzle based on this. For example, if BANANA = 30p and APPLE = 23p, what does a STRAWBERRY cost?
- If you give vowels and consonants different values, provide the words but not the value – challenge groups to work out how much the vowels and consonants are actually worth. For example, if ZEBRA = 36p, ELEPHANT = 57p, then how much is a WASP? (answer = 27p as vowels are worth 9p and consonants are worth 6p).

On the mark

On the mark is a decimal addition activity to help children improve adding decimal numbers with three decimal places.

Suitable for

KS2

Aims

- To add two or more decimal numbers with carrying.
- To understand place and face value.

Players

- An activity to be completed independently, in pairs or in small groups

Resources

- Paper and pencils (or whiteboard and pen)
- Decimal number box
- Calculators

What to do

- Give each pair a copy of the decimal number box shown here:
- Explain that you have some marking to do that you need help with.
- Show children the following:
  - i)   H + D = 8.858
  - ii) G + H = 8.55
  - iii) C + B = 0.992
  - iv) F + A + D + E = 50.338
  - v) B + F + A + A + D = 39.638

	Decimal number
A	4.42
B	0.89
C	0.012
D	3.208
E	18.7
F	24
G	2.9
H	5.65

- Ask children to add the decimal numbers that match each letter and work out which sums are correct and which are incorrect. Complete in pencil and paper first.
- After completing the sums, use a calculator to check whether your addition was right.
- Provide some similar examples for children to work out and set as a table challenge.

Variations

- Get children to invent their own decimal activity. Use some 0–9 digit cards and ask children to make some decimal numbers of their own. They can then add the decimal numbers and provide some mistakes of their own for another group to spot.
- Round each answer to its nearest whole tenth and nearest whole number.

Challenge questions

- Can you find which four numbers add up to:
  - i)   22.502 (answer = G+E+C=B),
  - ii) 17.716 (answer = H+H+D+D),
  - iii) 47.132 (C+A+F+E)

Plus trio

Plus trio is an addition game of strategy which focuses on adding numbers up to 65.

Suitable for

KS1
KS2

Aims

- To add single-digit numbers to 2-digit numbers.
- To understand place and face value.

Players

- A game for two players

Resources

- Paper and pencils (or whiteboard and pen)
- A Plus trio number grid
- A die labelled 28, 29, 30, 31, 32, 33
- Coloured counters

What to do

- Players get into pairs and decide who will be player A and player B.
- Give each pair a Plus trio number grid as shown here:

33	61	62	65	61	57
60	64	59	30	58	30
63	57	29	63	59	32
64	29	31	33	28	28
58	32	28	62	31	60

- Both players roll the die. Highest number starts.
- The first player rolls the die. The player is allowed to place counters on both numbers rolled or their sum. For example, if 28 and 29 are rolled then counters could be placed on 28 and 29 or on 57.
- The next player rolls the die and places counters or a counter on the number board but only if the numbers aren't covered.
- If a player cannot place a counter or counters then the next player rolls the dice.
- The first player to get three counters in a row horizontally, vertically or diagonally is the winner.

Variations

- You could change the numbers on the die to anything you wanted but the number grid would have to be changed too. For example, you could play this game with decimal numbers.
- The winner could be the first person to get three in a vertical line only.
- Rather than jumble all the numbers, these could be placed in order starting with the smallest in the bottom left corner.
- Play the game without the option of placing two counters on individual numbers thrown on the die – the numbers have to be added.

Challenge question

- Can you invent a different set of rules? For example, points are scored according to the numbers covered. If you make three in a row and one of your numbers is a square number then double your total.

Below bullseye

Below bullseye is an addition game which focuses on adding numbers up to 50.

Suitable for

KS1
KS2

Aims

- To add single-digit numbers to 2-digit numbers.
- To understand place and face value.

Players

- A game for three players

Resources

- Paper and pencils (or whiteboard and pen)
- A blank 3 x 3 number grid
- Coloured counters

What to do

- Organise children into groups of three. Player 1 is the leader.
- Give players 2 and 3 an empty 3 x 3 number grid each.
- Tell players 2 and 3 to fill each square with a number less than 50.
- The leader calls out an addition sum where the answer is less than 50.
- If player 1 or 2 has that number on their number grid then they cover it with a coloured counter.
- The winner is the first person to have all their numbers covered.
- The winner becomes the new leader.

Variations

- You could play this game for any number. Progress on to numbers less than 100.
- Try a 4 x 4 grid instead.
- Instead of addition try this as a subtraction game. You could play the game as an addition and subtraction game.

Challenge questions

- Can you invent a similar game using decimals as the focus? Would this game work as well? What decimals would you work with?
- Can you make a number cube so that all six sides contain nine numbers? This cube could then be used to play an addition/subtraction game whereby you roll the number cube and whichever face lands face up is the grid you play on.

It all adds up

It all adds up is an addition game with an element of risk and luck that children will enjoy playing.

Suitable for

KS1
KS2

Aims

- To add single-digit numbers to 2-digit numbers.
- To understand place and face value.

Players

- A game for two players.

Resources

- Paper and pencils (or whiteboard and pen)
- Two dice

What to do

- Each player needs a pencil and paper.
- Both players start at 0 and roll the dice to see who will go first. The highest or lowest number starts.
- Take it in turns to roll the dice as many times as you like in order to reach 65.
- Each time add the numbers you roll to your previous total and write it on your paper.
- You can choose to end your go at any time.
- If you roll a 4 then you lose your score for that go.
- The winner is the player who can make 65 or above.

Variations

- You can select any target number as appropriate.
- Play with three dice instead of two.
- Instead of 4 as a the 'lose your score' number, select another number.
- Rather than beginning the game at 0 you could start on a negative number, e.g. −10.
- Play this game as a multiplication game by making a product with the two dice thrown and increase the target number.
- Mix and match the operations. For example, you can decide to add or multiply when it is your throw.
- Dice numbers don't have to be 1–6. Relabel the faces with sticky labels with other numbers, e.g. you could have a prime number dice made up of 2, 3, 5, 7, 11, 13 and a composite number dice made up of 1, 4, 9, 16, 25, 36.

Challenge questions

- Can you think of a way of making the game more demanding? For example, the aim of the game could be to reach a target number in the fewest number of throws or the target number has to be reached exactly.
- Is there a penalty rule that would make the game riskier to play? For example, if you throw a double 1 you lose the whole of your score.

Spot 100

> Spot 100 is an enjoyable addition game using dominoes.

Suitable for

KS1
KS2

Aims

- To add 2-digit numbers.
- To understand place and face value.

Players

- A game for two players

Resources

- Paper and pencils (or whiteboard and pen)
- A set of dominoes

What to do

- Place a set of dominoes upside down on the table and shuffle them.
- Each player takes three dominoes and turns them over.
- Players now look at each domino to make three 2-digit numbers. Each domino can be treated as two 2-digit numbers (except for doubles). So, a domino with one spot and three spots could make 13 or 31.
- The aim of the game is to add the dominoes together to make 100 or as close to 100 as possible. For example, $46 + 24 + 31 = 101$.
- If a player makes an addition that equals exactly 100 then 100 points are scored. If a player can make a number 5 away from 100 then 20 points are scored. Any other number and no points are scored.
- Keep playing the game until all the dominoes run out.
- The player with the most points after all the dominoes have been used is the winner.

Variations

- You could use four dominoes instead of three to make 100.
- The target number could be more than or less than 100.
- You could play with two sets of dominoes, choose four dominoes and combine them to make two 4-digit numbers and play as close as possible to 10,000.
- You could invent new dominoes by placing sticky labels over the spots. For example, you could have numbers up to 9.

Challenge questions

- How many ways is it possible to make exactly 100 with three 2-digit numbers?
- Is it possible to make 100 with three prime numbers?
- Is it possible to make 100 with two primes and a square?

On a roll

On a roll is an addition game that assesses children's understanding of < and > in relation to number size.

Suitable for

KS1
KS2

Aims

- To add 2-digit numbers.
- To use and understand less than < and greater than > signs in order to win a game.

Players

- This game is best played in pairs.

Resources

- Paper and pencils (or whiteboard and pen)
- One die

What to do

- Get children to draw some empty addition and answer boxes on a piece of paper or on a whiteboard.
- Children take it in turns to roll a die 8 times (4 times each)
- After each roll players write down the number shown on the die in one of the boxes on their sheet or whiteboard.
- Tell children that after a number is written in a box it may not be changed.
- Children now find the two sums.

- If the number sentences about the sums are correct and

    both sums are 3-digit numbers = 10 points
    both sums are 2-digit numbers = 8 points
    only the larger sum is a 3-digit number = 4 points
    otherwise = 0 points

- Play the game three or four times. The player with the most points is the winner.

Variations

- You could add 3-digit numbers together and vary the number of rolls of the die.
- Adapt the point system, e.g. for an addition answer that is made up of prime numbers score 20 points.
- Instead of having a 1–6 die, place sticky labels over the spots and relabel from 4–9
- Round each answer to the nearest 100.

Challenge questions

- Does it make a difference where you place digits higher than 5?
- Are any of the addition sums multiples of 6? 7? 8? 9? What are the rules for divisibility for these numbers?

Fifteen

Fifteen is a game of addition and strategy involving thought, skill and luck.

Suitable for

KS1
KS2

Aims

- To make a total of 15 using three cards.
- To think strategically and outwit an opponent.

Players

- This game is best played in pairs.

Resources

- Paper and pencils (or whiteboards and pens)
- Digit cards 1–9 per pair

What to do

- Ask children to place the 1-9 cards in a row in front of them.
- Explain that the idea of the game is to add numbers together to make 15 using only three cards.
- Say that you can only take one card at a time.
- Demonstrate the game a few times so that children understand what to do. For example, 'If I choose 9 then what number should my opponent choose to stop me from making 15?'
- Play against a couple of children to illustrate the selection of numbers and tactics involved.

Variations

- Make 15 using any number of cards rather than 3.
- Instead of 15, select another number.
- Include more or less digit cards for different target numbers.

Challenge questions

- Does it matter who goes first? What is a fair way of deciding who goes first?
- What is the best strategy for winning the game?
- How many different ways of making 15 are there with the digit cards 1–9?

Three in a row

> Three in a row is a simple addition game combining strategy and luck.

Suitable for

KS1
KS2

Aims

- To make a target number using digit cards.
- To think strategically and outwit an opponent.

Players

- This game is best played in pairs.

Resources

- Paper and pencils (or whiteboards and pens)
- Digit cards 1–9 per pair

What to do

- Ask children to draw a 3 x 3 square grid.
- Shuffle the digit cards.
- Take it in turns to place the digits 1–9 in the grid.
- The only rule to keep in mind is that no one is allowed to open the game by placing 5 in the middle.
- The first player to get 3 numbers adding up to 15 is the winner.
- Play the game for an agreed number of times after which the player with the most points overall is the outright winner.

Variations

- Invent a new rule such as if you draw a 4, you get a free go.
- If you make 15 with two square numbers then you score 15 points extra.
- Invent a rule that no player can go in the middle square on the opening go.

Challenge questions

- Is there any advantage to going first?
- Is there a strategy to follow so that you will always win?
- How many different ways are there of making 15 using the numbers 1–9?

Palindromes

Palindromes is a fantastic activity for practising the addition of 3-digit numbers.

Suitable for

KS1
KS2

Aims

- To practise addition of 3-digit numbers.
- To understand what a palindromic number is.

Players

- An activity for one or two players

Resources

- Paper and pencil or whiteboard and pen
- Digit cards 0–9

What to do

- Deal three digit cards and write the numbers down on the whiteboard.
- Now reverse the digits and write these underneath.
- Add the two numbers together. For example,

$$\begin{array}{r} 216 \\ + \ 612 \\ \hline 828 \end{array}$$

- Explain to the class that a number that reads the same forwards as backwards is called a palindromic number so 828 is a palindromic number.

- Try another example on the board before children try themselves.
- Children can then try to find palindromic numbers themselves working independently or in pairs.

Variations

- Rather than use three cards, you could use more and investigate larger numbers.
- If a number is not palindromic, repeat the process. For example, if you deal 1, 5 and 4, reverse the digits and add you make 605. Rather than stop there, now reverse 605 and add. Does this make a palindromic number?

Challenge question

- Take some palindromic numbers. Can you always make them by adding a number and its reverse?

Fractured names

> Fractured names is a great activity for helping children to understand fractions and the concept of 'wholeness'.

Suitable for

KS1
KS2

Aims

- To practise adding fractions in order to make a whole.
- To recognise numerator and denominator and their meanings.

Players

- An activity for any number of participants

Resources

- Pencil and paper

What to do

- Get children to write down the name JAMES BOND.
- Now ask them to count all the letters that make up the whole name. There are 9 individual letters.
- Now explain that the whole can be broken into parts such as vowels and consonants.
- How many vowels out of 9 are there? There are 3 out of 9.
- How many consonants are there? There are 6 out of 9.
- Add the two parts together and what do you get? $3/9 + 6/9 = 9/9$
- Explain that this is another way of saying a whole because 9 divided by 9 is 1, that's one whole one.
- Now get children to investigate the fractional parts of their own names and those of their friends.

Variations

- Focus on specific maths vocabulary and use this for spelling activities centred around maths words.

Challenge questions

- Which names have the same fractional parts?
- Are there some names that don't make a whole?

In line

In line is an enjoyable game involving the addition of large numbers.

Suitable for

KS2

Aims

- To read and say large whole numbers.
- Know what each digit represents in terms of its place and face value.

Players

- A game for 2 players

Resources

- 1–6 die
- Coloured counters
- In line number grid and In line number boxes

What to do

- Give out the In line number board to children, one between two, as shown below:

In line number board

161, 621	221, 616	725, 401	7, 000	161, 916
110, 300	163, 616	5, 005	699, 957	725, 404
5, 002	110, 005	170, 000	759, 955	110, 002
700, 255	161, 618	727, 399	701, 955	785, 399
699, 960	5, 300	112, 000	65, 000	725, 699

In line number boxes

Box 1

1	2	3	4	5
2	5	300	2,000	60, 000

Box 2

1	2	3	4	5
5,000	110, 000	161, 616	699, 955	725, 399

- Take turns to roll the die. On your first roll, look under the number in Box 1 that matches your throw. For example, if you threw a 3 then your number is 300. Roll again to get your second number in Box 2.
- Now add the two numbers together and place a counter on the answer grid.
- If you roll a 6 then miss your turn.
- The winner is the first player to get three in a row.

Variations

- The numbers can be made smaller as appropriate.
- Include a game that includes six numbers rather than five remembering to add extra numbers to the answer grid.
- Keep a record of every number you cover to add up at the end of the game. Then find the digital root of the number. The player with the smallest digital root gets two extra turns in the next round of playing.

Challenge questions

- Can you round every number you cover to the nearest 1,000? 10,000? 100,000?
- Can you invent your own version of this game? Start by selecting six numbers to go in Box 1 and then six in Box 2. Add combinations of these together to fill a 5 x 5 grid.

Decimal roll

> Decimal roll is a game for adding decimals with three
> decimal places.

Suitable for

KS2

Aims

- Use standard column procedures to add and subtract integers and decimals.
- Know what each digit represents in terms of its place and face value.

Players

- A game for 2 players

Resources

- 1–6 die
- Decimal roll number sheet

What to do

- Children get into pairs.
- Give out a copy of the Decimal roll sheet to each player and explain
  how to play the game (draw a whole number square, a decimal point,
  a tenth square, a hundredth square x 2, one above the other)
- Players take it in turns to roll a die eight times.
- After each roll, players write the number thrown in one of the empty
  squares.
- When the squares have been filled, both players add their decimal
  numbers together.
- Score the number you need to add to your total to make the next
  whole number. For example, if you made 6.25 and 4.61 then this
  would make 10.86. To make 10.86 into 11, the next whole number,
  you would need 0.14 so 0.14 is your score.
- The winner is the player with the largest total after three rounds.

Variations

- Play the game to include thousandths.
- The player with the smallest total after five rounds is the winner.
- If your digital root is five then your score doesn't count.
- Play this as a subtraction game.
- Use different numbered dice.

Challenge questions

- Can you write the number you have made?
- Can you add 1, add 10, add 100, add 0.1, add 0.01 to the number you have made?
- Can you invent some new rules for the game?

Chapter 3
Subtraction

My difference

My difference is a game to help children find the difference between 2- and 3-digit numbers.

Suitable for

KS2

Aims

- To subtract combinations of 3- and 2-digit numbers.
- To refine calculation methods.

Players

- This game is for small groups of three or four.

Resources

- My difference number board
- Pencil and paper

What to do

- Give each pair of players a copy of the My difference number grid shown here

164	74	138	90
115	104	55	59
38	124	139	49
64	80	63	99
79	88	54	113

- Explain that the aim of the activity is to find as many pairs of numbers as possible with a difference of 25. For example, $164 - 139 = 25$.
- Challenge groups to find as many as they can.
- The group with the most pairs after 5 minutes are the winners.

Variations

- You could make this game simpler by including smaller numbers and having a difference of 9.
- You could add layers to the grid by including more rows of numbers, some with a difference of 25.
- You could choose a different 'difference' number using the same grid. For example, how many pairs of numbers have a difference of 61.

Challenge question

- Can you invent number sentences or a number problem that match the numbers you have subtracted? For example, a library bookshelf had 104 books on it at the beginning of the week. After three days it has 14 fewer books. How many books are on the shelf now?

What a pair

What a pair is a game to help children subtract decimal numbers with one decimal place.

Suitable for

KS2

Aims

- To subtract combinations of decimal numbers with one decimal place or more.
- To refine calculation methods.

Players

- This game is for two players

Resources

- What a pair number grid
- Pencil and paper

What to do

- Give each pair of players a number grid as follows

6.2	5.3	4.4	4.1	1.6
2.9	2.6	1.7	4.2	1.8
2.7	2.8	5.2	5.4	6.1
1.9	4.3	3.6	6.2	3.7

- Now ask children to cut the grid into individual number cards.
- Shuffle the cards and place them face down on the table.
- Players take turns to take two cards each. If they have a difference of 2.5 then they add the numbers together to achieve their score. For example, 5.4 − 2.9 = 2.5. This player would score 5.4 + 2.9 = 8.3

- If the numbers don't have a difference of 2.5 then place to one side.
- When all the cards have been used, any cards left in a pile, shuffle again and continue the game.
- The player with the most points after 10 minutes of playing or when the cards run out is the winner.

Variations

- You could play this game with more cards or fewer cards depending on the class and groups within.
- Change the difference from 2.5 to another decimal number. For example, 3.6.
- Have different points for particular differences. For example, a difference of 2.5 = 2 points, a difference of 0.1 = 5 points, a difference of 2.4 = 10 points.
- You could play this game in the style of 'Pelmanisim' and lay the cards out in a 4 x 5 grid so that the cards are placed face down. This way, children have to remember where the cards are on the grid.

Challenge questions

- Can you play this game where there is a penalty for selecting certain numbers? For example, if you select two cards where the tenths digit is the same then you lose all your points.
- Can you invent this game for numbers with more than one decimal place?

What a difference!

> **What a difference! is a game to help children subtract 2-digit numbers from 4-digit numbers.**

Suitable for

KS2

Aims

- To subtract combinations of 2-digit numbers from 4-digit whole numbers.
- To refine calculation methods.

Players

- This game is for 2 players.

Resources

- What a difference number grid
- Pencil and paper

What to do

- Show the class the following number grid:

5624	5512	5530	5523	5225
5508	5607	5561	5232	5055
5590	5589	5539	5522	5505
5563	5573	5556	5252	5448
5574	5540	5555	5625	**5471**

- Explain that the aim of the game is to move through the grid from the number in the top left corner to the number in the bottom left corner by subtracting 17 each time. The numbers are connected but not all of them. Explain that the numbers have to be adjacent to each other. Explain the word adjacent. For example, $5624 - 17 = 5607$, so 5607 can be shaded in. Which number comes next? Show the class the route through the grid after you have given everyone a chance to work out the subtractions. The route through will look like this:

5624	5512	5530	5523	5225
5508	5607	5561	5232	5055
5590	5589	5552	5539	5522
5563	5573	5556	5252	5505
5574	5540	5555	5625	5471

- Players now pair up and receive the same grid and it is a race to see how many can find a route from the starting number to the end. Choose a different number to subtract each time. Use 23 in this example,

2541	2248	2054	2398	2566
2482	2428	2540	2382	2481
2539	2824	2405	2359	2538
2804	2679	2240	2336	2338
2123	2583	2244	2337	2313

- The first player to have correctly shaded in a route of numbers from the start to the end is the winner.
- Now use different grids and practise subtracting different numbers.

Variations

- Use a bigger or smaller grid as appropriate with a trail of numbers beginning at a different point on the grid, e.g. first column second square down.
- Increase or decrease the numbers inside the squares to suit the level appropriate to the group/class.
- To make the 'difference' number, shuffle a pack of 0–9 playing cards and then take two numbers to make a 2-digit number.

Challenge questions

- Look at the number grid – can you find the largest and smallest numbers and then subtract them?
- Can you add all the numbers in one row and subtract them from the numbers in the bottom row?
- Look at the numbers inside each square – can you split them to make two 2-digit numbers and subtract them?
- Can you find a route through the grid in under 2 minutes?
- Can you invent your own number trail grid?

In order

In order is a game to help children subtract decimal numbers with two decimal places.

Suitable for

KS2

Aims

- To subtract combinations of decimal numbers with two or more decimal places.
- To refine calculation methods.

Players

- This game is for 2 players

Resources

- 3 dice per player
- Pencil and paper

What to do

- Write three numbers on the board and place a decimal point between them. For example, 7.45.
- Now roll a dice three twice. Explain that your first throw gives the number of hundredths, your second throw gives the number of tenths and the third row gives the number of units.
- For example, if you throw 351 then the number made will be 1.53 and this number is then subtracted from 7.45 to make 5.92.
- This can be practised a few more times so that children get familiar with the game.
- Now write some decimal numbers on the board which children will use to subtract from: 8.99, 5.28, 4.01, 2.56, etc.
- Players then take it in turns to subtract their dice rolls from the numbers on the board.
- The first player to make a total of more than 20 is the winner.

Variations

- You could play this game with decimal numbers with one just decimal place and two throws of the dice.
- Play with tens, units and tenths.
- Play with a 4–9 die instead (this may mean that you have to swap the top number and bottom numbers over in order to subtract them).
- The first player to make 50 is the winner.
- When you have worked out your subtraction, your answer becomes the new number to start with.

Challenge questions

- Can you read the numbers you have made?
- Can you round the numbers to the nearest tenth? hundredth?
- Can you reverse the digits to make a new subtraction? Does this make a bigger or smaller number?

Take it away

Take it away is a game to help children subtract a 3-digit whole number from a 4-digit whole number.

Suitable for

KS2

Aims

- To subtract combinations of 3 and 4-digit whole numbers.
- To refine calculation methods.

Players

- This game is for 2 players

Resources

- 3 dice per player
- Pencil and paper

What to do

- Explain what to do with the whole class first. Write the following number on the board and ask children to write it on their paper: 7922.
- Now ask children to roll three dice to make a 3-digit number.
- Challenge the class to identify the types of number thrown. For example, if 3, 4, 5 are thrown then 3 = a prime number, 4 = a composite number, 5 = a prime number.
- Players now subtract the 3-digit number from 7922 using a pencil and paper method to get 7577. The digital root of this number is then the score. So, 7 + 5 + 7 + 7 = 26, 2 + 6 = 8, so 8 is scored.
- Now write some 4-digit numbers on the board for children to work with: 8654, 9023, 1352, 6767, 5499, 8921, etc.
- The player with the highest score after 9 turns is the winner.

Variations

- Players make as many 3-digit numbers as they can with the dice thrown and subtract this from the 4-digit number.
- Players could throw two dice and subtract from a 3-digit number or throw one die and subtract from a 2-digit number.
- Rather than find the digital root, players could be award points if their answer is even, odd, contains three prime numbers, etc.

Challenge questions

- Can you think of another way to generate the starting numbers? For example, using a 0–9 spinner.
- Can you make the game more challenging? For example, what about using 5- or 6-digit numbers to subtract from?
- How many different ways could you subtract? Use more than one method and compare them.

Spot on

> **Spot on is a game to help children subtract 2-digit whole numbers.**

Suitable for

KS1
KS2

Aims

- To subtract combinations of two 2-digit whole numbers.
- To refine calculation methods.

Players

- This game is for 2 players

Resources

- Dominoes
- Pencil and paper

What to do

- Give each pair of players a set of dominoes.
- Mix the dominoes up and place them face down on the table.
- Players take one domino each and the lowest number starts the game.
- The starting player then takes a domino and makes two 2-digit numbers. For example, 2 spots and 4 spots would make 42 and 24. The two numbers are then subtracted to make 18.
- The number made is the score for that player. Players keep playing and totalling the scores they make.
- The first player to make 200 is the winner.

Variations

- Players could take two dominoes and make a subtraction with them.
- Players could take two dominoes and make two 4-digit numbers to subtract.
- A domino taken could be multiplied by 5 to make a bigger number.

Challenge questions

- What do you notice about dominoes that are doubles? Is it fair to include these numbers?
- Is there anything you notice about the differences? Do they make even numbers? odd numbers? both?
- Could you turn this into a fraction game? For example, take two dominoes and use the dots to make fractions. So, 2 dots and 5 dots would make $\frac{2}{5}$. Players can then take this fraction away from 1 whole.

Play your cards right

> Play your cards right is a game to help children subtract decimal numbers.

Suitable for

KS2

Aims

- To subtract combinations of decimal numbers with two decimal places.
- To refine calculation methods.

Players

- This game is for 2 players

Resources

- Playing cards
- Pencil and paper

What to do

- Give each pair of players a pack of playing cards – players only need 1-9 cards.
- Shuffle the cards and place them in a pile on the table.
- Each player takes three cards.
- Players then make a decimal number with as big a difference as possible from 10. For example, $10 - 2.95 = 7.05$
- Players score according to the number they make.
- The winner is the first player to get over 25.

Variations

- Players can get the number nearest to 10 rather than find the biggest difference.
- Play the greatest difference from 12.
- Play the game with the picture cards which can act as jokers worth any number the player wishes.
- Include 0 digit cards.

Challenge questions

- Can you play the game with four cards and subtract from 10? For example, $10 - 1.256 = 8.744$
- Can you round your answer up or down to the nearest tenth?

On the grid

On the grid is a game to help children subtract two 2-digit numbers.

Suitable for

KS2

Aims

- To subtract combinations of 2-digit numbers.
- To refine calculation methods.

Players

- This game is for 2 players

Resources

- 1–100 number grid
- 0–9 digit cards
- Coloured counters
- Pencil and paper

What to do

- Give each pair of players a copy of the 1–100 grid shown on page 84.
- Shuffle two sets of 0–9 digits and place them in a pile on the table.
- Each player takes a card and the highest number starts.
- The first player then takes four cards and makes two 2-digit numbers.
- The smaller number is then subtracted from the larger. If the number made is on the grid then cover with a counter.
- The first player to get five counters in a row is the winner.

1	2	3	4	5	6	7	8	9	10
11	12	13	14	15	16	17	18	19	20
21	22	23	24	25	26	27	28	29	30
31	32	33	34	35	36	37	38	39	40
41	42	43	44	45	46	47	48	49	50
51	52	53	54	55	56	57	58	59	60
61	62	63	64	65	66	67	68	69	70
71	72	73	74	75	76	77	78	79	80
81	82	83	84	85	86	87	88	89	90
91	92	93	94	95	96	97	98	99	100

Variations

- Play the game with a smaller number square.
- Play the game as an addition and subtraction game.
- The first player to get a counter in each row is the winner.
- The first player to cover two square numbers, two primes and two composites is the winner.

Challenge questions

- How many numbers have you covered that have three factors?
- How many numbers have you covered that have a digital root of 2?
- Are there any numbers it is impossible to make?
- Could you play this game with three cards?

Take cover

Take cover is a game to help children subtract with decimals to two decimal places.

Suitable for

KS2

Aims

- To subtract combinations of decimal numbers involving tenths and hundredths.
- To refine calculation methods.

Players

- This game is for 2 players

Resources

- Take cover number board
- Decimal digit cards
- Coloured counters
- Pencil and paper
- Calculators

What to do

- Give each pair a copy of the Take cover number board shown on page 86.
- Give each pair the following decimal digit cards: 0.1, 0.1, 0.25, 0.25, 0.5, 0.5, 0.75, 0.75, 1, 1, 1.25, 1.25, 1.5, 1.5, 1.75, 1.75, 2, 2.
- Shuffle the decimal cards and place them face down on the table.

0.85	0.35	1.15	1.25	1.5	2
1.5	2	0.25	1.75	2.75	0.15
1.85	1.6	0.6	2.25	3	0.9
2.5	0.25	0.35	1	1.5	0.7
0.25	0.4	3.75	2.5	0.25	1
2.5	3	1	3.5	1.4	2.1

- Decide who goes first. The first player then takes two cards and subtracts the numbers to make a number on the decimal number grid. For example,
  1.25 − 0.75 = 0.5.
- If a number can be made on the grid, place a counter on that number.
- After each go, the cards are placed to one side.
- The player with the most counters after playing for ten minutes is the winner.

Variations

- Play the game as an addition and subtraction game.
- Play the game where the winner is the first to get four in a row.
- Play the game with a smaller grid, e.g. 4 x 4.
- Remove the 0.1 cards from the digit card pile.

Challenge questions

- Can you make a game that is more challenging? For example, make some cards from 0.1 to 0.9 and invent some new numbers for a 6 x 6 grid.
- Can you add all the numbers you have covered and subtract them from the total of your opponent?

Stepping stones

Stepping stones is a game to help children mentally subtract one 2-digit number from another 2-digit number.

Suitable for

KS2

Aims

- To subtract combinations of 2-digit numbers.
- To refine calculation methods.

Players

- This game is for 2 players

Resources

- Stepping stones number tracks
- Pencil and paper
- A 1–6 die
- Coloured counters

What to do

- Each player in a pair is given a copy of the same Stepping stones number track shown here.

| 61 | 44 | 94 | 65 | 23 | 46 | 92 | 33 | 25 | 35 | 63 |

- Now write the following numbers on the board: 96, 38, 67, 29, 36, 69, 47, 97, 66, 48.

- Players take it in turns to roll the die. They then choose a number from those written on the board and subtract. If the number they have made is a number on their Stepping stone track then they cover the number with a counter. If they cannot cover a number then it is the turn of the next player.
- The winner is the player who covers all of the numbers on the Stepping stone track.

Variations

- Play the game with more stepping stones and repeat some of the numbers.
- Invent a whole new line of numbers for the board and work out the differences between them in order to complete a new Stepping stones track.

Challenge questions

- Can you invent a game where two dice are used to perform a subtraction?
- Can you make this game more challenging by including 4-digit numbers?
- Can you identify which numbers you have covered are squares? Composites? Primes?

All in a line

All in a line is a game to help children subtract one 3-digit number from another 3-digit number.

Suitable for

KS2

Aims

- To subtract combinations of 3-digit numbers.
- To refine calculation methods.

Players

- This game is for 2 players

Resources

- All in a line number grid
- Pencil and paper
- Coloured counters

What to do

- Each pair of players is given a copy of the All in a line number grid shown here.

653	861	561	438	750
785	323	485	459	482
674	535	574	334	764
274	593	133	621	393
252	367	693	367	467

- Now write on the grid the following rows of numbers:
    868, 965, 697, 797, 889, 678
    404, 104, 430, 344, 215, 545
- Tell children that they have to select a number from the top row and a number from the bottom row, find the difference and then cover the number made on the board if it is there.
- The winner is the first player to cover 7 squares.

Variations

- This game could be played with bigger or smaller numbers.
- Try making a new board with a mixture of 2-digit and 3-digit numbers.
- Increase the board size from a 5 x 5 to something smaller or larger.
- The first to cover four numbers with a digital root of 4 wins the game.

Challenge questions

- Can you make up a similar game for subtracting decimals?
- How fair is the game? Are there any number differences not represented on the board?
- Would it matter if the numbers on the board were placed in ascending order?

Blockbusters

> **Blockbusters is a challenging activity designed to help practise subtraction and estimation skills.**

Suitable for

KS2

Aims

- To subtract combinations of 1- and 2-digit numbers.
- To refine calculation methods.

Players

- This game is for 2 players

Resources

- Blockbuster grid
- Pencil and paper
- Coloured counters

What to do

- Each pair is given a blockbuster-style grid of hexagons shown here and on page 92.

  5 rows of hexagons
  1st row = 6 hexagons across
  2nd row = 5 hexagons across
  3rd row = 6 hexagons across
  4th row = 5 hexagons across
  5th row = 6 hexagons across

1st row of numbers as follows (69, 28, 9, 22, 15, 24)
2nd row (11, 17, 32, 56, 47)
3rd row (21, 37, 9, 26, 35, 13)
4th row (31, 48, 6, 34, 18)
5th row (13, 19, 8, 43, 56, 25)

- Write on the board the following numbers: 15, 28, 36, 47, 53, 62, 71, 84.
- Players take it in turns to select two numbers from the board to make a number on the Blockbuster grid. If the difference between the two numbers can be made then place a counter on the grid. For example, 84 − 62 = 22.
- The winner is the player who can make a chain of hexagons which connects either left to right or top to bottom.

Variations

- This game could be played with more hexagons and numbers.
- Select larger starting numbers (e.g. the 8 numbers you write on the board) and calculate their differences for placing inside the Blockbuster grid.
- Use a calculator for checking differences.

Challenge question

- Can you make up other grids for different numbers or for different operations?

Hey big spender

> **Hey big spender is a calculator subtraction activity involving money.**

Suitable for

KS2

Aims

- To subtract combinations of 3-digit numbers.
- To refine calculation methods.

Players

- This game is for 2–4 players

Resources

- Paper and pencils (or whiteboards and pens)
- A calculator
- 3 dice

What to do

- Each player has a pretend £100 to spend.
- Players take it in turns to roll three dice and then make a 3-digit number. For example, £6.15.
- The amount made is then taken away from £100 using a calculator.
- Players keep a record of what they have thrown and how much they have left on paper.
- Play continues until one player gets below £5.00.

Variations

- This game can be played with numbered dice labelled 4–9.
- Select a different starting amount, e.g. £75, £150, etc.
- Roll a die three times. The first throw equals the number of pounds, the second throw equals the 'tens' of pence and the next throw equals the 'units' of pence.
- Play this game without a calculator.
- The first player to reach less than £10, £2, etc.

Challenge questions

- Can you play this game with four dice and subtract the amounts made from £1,000?
- Can you suggest things you could actually purchase with the amount thrown? For example, £14.25, a new T-shirt.
- Do you recognise how to combine the dice to reduce the amount more quickly?

Make a difference

Make a difference is a simple subtraction and addition game that involves making numbers up to 12.

Suitable for

KS1

Aims

- To add or subtract mentally combinations of 1-digit and 2-digit numbers.
- To refine calculation methods.

Players

- This game is for 2 players

Resources

- Paper and pencils (or whiteboards and pens)
- A 3 x 4 number grid
- Coloured counters
- Two dice

What to do

- Pair children into partners and give them a 3 x 4 grid. Children could draw this themselves.
- Explain to children that the aim of the game is to cover as many numbers on the grid as possible.
- Tell children that they have to throw two dice and then either add the numbers or subtract them in order to make a number from 1 to 12. For example, throwing a 3 and a 4 could be 4-3 = 1 or 3 + 4 = 7.
- When a number has been made then the number is covered with a coloured counter. Once a number has been covered, the counter cannot be removed until the end of the game.

- The winner is the player who has covered the most numbers at the end of the game.
- In case of a tie, then players add the numbers they have covered and the winner is the player with the largest total.

Variations

- This game can be extended by including more number squares and using more dice.
- Relabel one die from 6 to 11 with sticky labels.
- Instead of a grid, a number line from 1 to 12 could be used with bonus points achieved for covering 1 and 12.
- You could adapt this game for multiplication.
- Instead of having a rule where a counter cannot be removed, allow children to remove an opponent's counter if they make that number.

Challenge questions

- Can you renumber the dice and make this game more challenging?
- Can you make a rule that rewards players for landing on a particular number?
- Does including another player in the game make it harder or easier?
- Is the game more enjoyable with more numbers?

What's the difference?

> What's the difference? is a place value and subtraction game using 5-digit numbers.

Suitable for

KS2

Aims

- To provide practice in making 5-digit numbers in subtraction.
- To recognise place value and build confidence finding the difference between large numbers.

Players

- This game is for 2–4 players.

Resources

- Paper and pencils (or whiteboards and pens)
- Pack of 45 digit cards, 5 each of the digits 1–9

What to do

- Shuffle the cards and deal 10 to each player.
- Explain to children that the aim of the game is to make the highest possible number from 5 of the 10 cards and the lowest possible number from the other 5.
- Each player then subtracts the lowest number from the highest number (using a pencil and paper method).
- The player with the greatest difference is the winner.

- Provide an example before the children play on their own, e.g.

  Player 1 receives 3, 6, 5, 2, 3, 9, 7, 1, 9 and 6
  Highest number 99,766
  Lowest number 12,335

  Difference 87,431

  Player 2 receives 2, 9, 1, 6, 5, 5, 4, 3, 1, 2
  Highest number 96,554
  Lowest number 11,223

  Difference 85,331

  Player 1 is the winner by 2,100

Variations

- Make the game easier by using fewer cards or more demanding with more cards.
- Make pairs of numbers with the smallest possible difference.

Challenge questions

- Can you invent bonus points for the game? For example, if the difference is divisible by 6 then score an extra 50 points.
- Can you invent any penalty point rules? For example, if your difference contains any prime numbers then score 20 points less per prime.

What difference does it make?

What difference does it make? provides practice in making 5-digit numbers and in subtraction.

Suitable for

KS2

Aims

- To provide practice in making 5-digit numbers in subtraction.
- To practise subtracting large numbers.

Players

- This game is for 2–4 players

Resources

- Paper and pencils (or whiteboards and pens)
- Pack of 45 digit cards, 5 each of the digits 1–9

What to do

- Shuffle the cards and deal ten to each player.
- Tell children to turn over their cards to make the highest possible 5-digit number they can and the lowest possible 5-digit number they can.
- Each player subtracts the smallest number from the biggest.
- The winner is the player with the greatest difference. For example,

    Player 1 receives 3, 5, 1, 3, 9, 2, 5, 6, 7, 2

    Highest number = 97,655
    Lowest number = 12,233

    Difference = 85,422

Player 2 receives 9,4,8,5,6,2,6,7,1,2

Highest number = 98,766
Lowest number = 12,245

Difference = 86,521

Player 2 is the winner by 1,099.

- Points are scored according to the difference. So, in the example above 1,099 points are scored.
- Play this game for five rounds to find an overall winner.

Variations

- Play the game with a smaller number of cards, e.g. deal players six cards each to make two 3-digit numbers.
- Award bonus points for any difference that is a palindromic number such as 1001.
- Play the game using only odd digits or even digits.
- Include joker cards in your pack of digit cards so that the card assumes any value.
- Play the game where the aim is to make the smallest possible difference.

Challenge question

- When the aim of the game is to make the smallest possible difference, do you have to make two large numbers and then subtract them or two small numbers and then subtract them?

Dicey difference

Dicey difference is a subtraction game determined by the roll of a die.

Suitable for

KS1
KS2

Aims

- To use knowledge of addition and subtraction facts and place value to derive sums and differences between 2-digit numbers.

Players

- This game is for 2 players

Resources

- Paper and pencils (or whiteboards and pens)
- A 6 x 6 number grid plus 'Number roll' strip
- Coloured counters
- One 1–6 die

What to do

- Players get into pairs ready to start.
- Give out copies of the number grid and 'number roll' strip as shown here.
- The first player throws a die. If a three is thrown then the player chooses one number underneath the three column as shown in the number strip.

Number grid

16	29	23	22	61	19
11	25	44	66	54	22
21	38	66	15	23	62
32	55	50	61	25	63
47	53	34	44	40	22
17	29	22	33	60	15

Number roll strip

1	2	3	4	5	6
91	70	80	48	50	78
30	46	16	60	77	25
27	78	63	16	91	25

- The first player rolls again and whatever number is thrown, a number underneath is chosen again.
- The two numbers chosen are then made into a subtraction sum. If the difference appears on the number board then this number can be covered with a coloured counter.
- Now throw the die again. If you throw a six then you can remove an opponent's counter.
- If a number cannot be made then miss a go.
- Players take it in turns until one player can make four in a row either vertically, horizontally or diagonally.

Variations

- This game can be adapted for larger numbers. Choose a grid size and then fill it with numbers of your choice. Numbers on the number strip will need to be combinations of numbers which when subtracted make the numbers on the number board.
- Play three in a row or five in a row as alternatives.

Challenge questions

- Can you think of a way of making 18 numbers for the Number roll strip? For example, these can be made by dealing out 0–9 digit cards in order to make the numbers.
- When you have made 18 numbers, can you subtract the numbers from each other to ensure the number board is filled? Are there enough numbers to fill the board? Are there too many? If there are, what is the fairest way of not including some of the subtraction combinations you have made?

Big difference

Big difference is a subtraction game that helps children to practise subtracting decimal numbers with three decimal places.

Suitable for

KS2

Aims

- To use efficient written methods to add and subtract integers and decimals.
- To subtract decimal numbers up to three decimal places.

Players

- This game is for 2-4 players.

Resources

- Paper and pencils (or whiteboards and pens)
- 0–9 digit cards

What to do

- Each pair or group get two sets of 0–9 digit cards.
- Shuffle the cards. Players take it in turns to take six digit cards and then make two decimal numbers with two decimal places. For example, 6.32 and 5.69.
- The smallest decimal number is subtracted from the largest.
- The digits of the answer are then added together in order to find the digital root. Remind children that to find the digital root add the digits, then add the digits of the total until you reach a 1-digit number. So, in the example above 6.32 – 5.69 = 0.63. The digital root of 0.63 is 0 + 6 + 3 = 9, so 9 points are scored.
- Play continues like this until everyone has had three turns each. The winner is the player who has scored most points.

Variations

- Play the game with numbers that have three decimal places.
- Alter the point system. For example, score points to match each digit in the answer which is greater than 5. So, in the example above, 0.63 would have scored 6 points.

Challenge questions

- Can you round each answer to the nearest tenth?
- Can you round each answer to the nearest whole number?
- Can you name the place and face value of each digit in the answer?

Chapter 4
Multiplication

Gridlock

Gridlock is a multiplication game for helping children with their times tables as well as practising their problem-solving skills.

Suitable for

KS2

Aims

- Rapid recall of multiplication facts.
- Know by heart all multiplication facts up to 10 x 10.

Players

- A game for the whole class

Resources

- One ordinary die
- Product grids

What to do

- Give everyone a copy of the grid shown here.

	24	36	48	score
6				
20				
30				
score				

- Throw the die and announce the number thrown.
- Pupils then place the number thrown in one of the nine boxes on their grid.

- Continue rolling the die until all the boxes have been filled.
- A number cannot be changed once it has been placed in a box.
- Score 5 points for each time a row or column heading is the product of the three numbers in that row or column. For example, 6, 1 and 4 make 24 in the first column so that is 5 points. 6, 2 and 1 in the first row make 12 so that is also 5 points giving a bottom right-hand corner total of 10.

	24	36	48	score
6	6	2	1	5
20	1	5	4	0
30	4	4	2	0
score	5	0	0	10

- Play several games together and see who can collect the most points out of all the games played.

Variations

- Investigate using numbers in the range 1–9.
- Try different product headings.
- Investigate arrangements which will give a score of 15.

Challenge question

- What is the maximum score you could get for the grid above if you rearranged the numbers?

Four in a row

Four in a row is a great game for helping children learn their multiplication tables.

Suitable for

KS2

Aims

- Rapid recall of multiplication facts.
- Know by heart all multiplication facts up to 10 x 10.

Players

- A game for two or three players

Resources

- Two dice, one labelled 3, 4, 5, 6, 7, 8 and the other marked 4, 5, 6, 7, 8, 9
- Coloured counters
- 4 in a row multiplication board

What to do

- Get children into pairs and give them a copy of the four in a row number grid shown on page 111.
- Decide who will go first.
- One player rolls the dice and finds the product.
- If the product can be found on the number board then cover that number with a counter.
- If the number you have made isn't on the board then wait until your next turn.
- The winner is the first player to get four in a row.

35	64	24	28	63	20	42	64	20	18
30	24	32	35	32	24	30	40	30	24
15	45	48	72	36	30	16	24	24	49
35	35	36	42	18	24	24	36	40	56
48	15	28	27	48	40	30	24	42	45
24	24	56	56	20	15	12	16	63	24
81	54	32	24	56	48	20	28	20	32
56	21	21	15	72	56	56	24	40	21
40	20	32	24	54	25	35	12	35	36
32	12	24	72	24	20	56	28	25	48

Variations

- The number grid could be made bigger or smaller to include more or fewer numbers.
- Play with four dice and make two separate products to cover.
- Play five in a row.

Challenge questions

- Are all the numbers fairly represented? Do some numbers appear more than once? Have some numbers been missed out?
- Can you think of a rule for making the game more challenging? For example, the winner is the player who gets four numbers in a row where the units digit is an even number or a prime number.

Funky factors

Funky factors is an interactive game activity for helping children identify factors and multiples.

Suitable for

KS2

Aim

- Use knowledge of place value and multiplication facts to 10 x 10, the corresponding division facts and multiples of numbers to 10 up to the tenth multiple.

Players

- A game for two or three players

Resources

- Two 1–6 dice
- Coloured counters
- Funky factors sheet

What to do

- Organise children into appropriate groupings. Mixed ability will work best.
- Give children a copy of the Funky factors sheet shown here.

120	27	18	50	35
28	72	44	25	12
33	24	45	21	9
32	42	15	14	48

- Players take it in turns to throw two dice and add up the score.
- If the number made is a factor of a number on the board then cover that number with a counter. For example, if you made 8 you could cover 24 because 8 x 3 = 24, so 8 is a factor of 24.
- If you cannot make a number on the grid then the next player takes their turn.
- The winner is the player to cover any five squares.

Variations

- Increase the grid size to include more numbers.
- Throw three dice and add them together.
- Throw four dice; add three dice and subtract one of them.
- Score points according to the number covered and then add all squares covered after playing for five minutes.

Challenge questions

- Can you write all the factors of the number you have covered?
- Can you invent a version of the game so that all the numbers on the board have four factors?

A finger in every pie

A finger in every pie is an activity for helping children multiply single-digit numbers together to find a range of products.

Suitable for

KS1
KS2

Aims

- To develop multiplication facts up to 10 x 10.

Players

- A game for two players

Resources

- Six 1–6 dice
- Coloured counters
- A finger in every pie sheet

What to do

- Organise children into small groups and give them a copy of the activity sheet on page 115.
- The first player rolls the six dice and then splits them into three groups of two.
- One group of dice is put to one side and ignored.
- The remaining groups are added and multiplied. For example, if a player rolled 5, 6; 2, 4; 3, 2 then 3, 2 are put to one side. 5 and 6 are added to make 11 and 2 and 4 are added to make 6. 11 and 6 are then multiplied together to make 66.
- Players place a counter on the product made.
- The winner is the first player to get a counter in every pie.

- If a player cannot place a counter on a pie then their opponent takes their turn.
- Once a counter has been placed it cannot be removed.

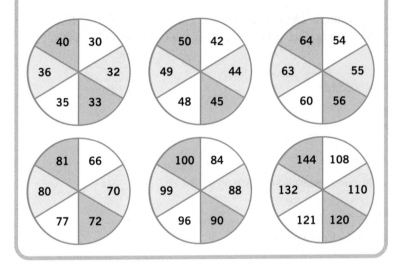

Variations

- Play with four dice so that players have to work with the numbers thrown.
- Play with 4–9 dice.
- The winner could be the first player to cover a whole pie.
- Counters can be removed if an opponent makes the covered number when it is their turn.
- Increase the number of slices each pie has to eight to include more numbers.

Challenge questions

- If you used two 4–9 dice what numbers would you have to place inside the pies?
- Could you play this game with eight 1–6 dice? What rules would you change?
- Could you include more than six pies?
- Would the game be harder or easier to play with fewer pies?

Multiple choices

> Multiple choices is an activity for helping children find and use factors whilst improving their multiplication skills.

Suitable for

KS1
KS2

Aims

- To develop multiplication facts up to 10 x 10.

Players

- A game for two players

Resources

- Two 1–6 dice
- Multiple choices number grids
- Pencil and paper

What to do

- Players team up with a maths buddy.
- Give each pair a copy of the Multiple choices board shown here.

	6	7	9	Score
2				
3				
4				
Score				

- Players take turns to roll both dice. Players then make a two-digit number from the numbers thrown. For example, 3 and 6 could make 36 or 63.
- Each player then writes the number thrown in one of the spaces on their Factor fun board.
- Players score a point if the number is a multiple of either of the set of numbers above and to the left of the space chosen.
- If it is a multiple of both numbers then three points are scored. For example, 36 could be placed in the square below because it is a multiple of 4 and 9.

	6	7	9	Score
2				
3				
4			36	3
Score			3	

- If you threw a 2 and a 1 to make 21 then it would score just one point if placed in the square as shown here

	6	7	9	Score
2				
3				
4		21	36	3
Score		1	3	

- Players keep taking turns until all the spaces are filled.
- When all the spaces have been filled add the points of each row and column to get a total.
- The player with the highest total is the winner.

Variations

- This game can be played with players completing two boards at the same time or a larger version of the Multiple choices board.
- Play this game as a factor game. For example, players each have a copy of the board shown here.

	9	16	25	Score
10				
24				
36				
Score				

- Players then throw one die and they write the number thrown in one of the spaces on the board. So if someone threw a 5 then the best place to put that would be as follows, scoring 6 points in total.

	9	16	25	Score
10			5	3
24				
36				
Score			3	

Challenge questions

- Can you think of another way of generating the numbers that go into the number boards? For example, you could use 0–9 digit cards.
- Can you think of a different scoring system? For example, if your total score has four factors, then multiply your score by 4.

Times square

Times square is an activity for helping introduce children with their multiplication facts up to 6 x 6.

Suitable for

KS1
KS2

Aims

- To develop multiplication facts up to 6 x 6.
- To use precise mathematical statements when describing multiplication facts.

Players

- Small groups or pairs

Resources

- Two 1–6 dice
- Times square number grid
- Coloured counters

What to do

- Give each pair a copy of the Times square number shown here.

3	18	36	15	1	2
6	5	20	12	2	9
18	8	6	8	30	5
25	12	10	4	4	16
20	4	3	12	24	24
12	10	15	30	6	6

- Players take it in turns to throw two dice and multiply together.
- The product of the two numbers is then covered on the Times square grid. Players say aloud the multiplication they have made. For example, 'The product of six threes is eighteen', rather than just 18.
- The winner is the first player to get a block of four squares.

Variations

- Change the game to include facts up to 9 x 9 using dice labelled 4–9 with corresponding multiplication facts represented on the number board.
- Rather than a block of four, players have to get four in a row.
- Use three dice where players have a choice to keep two out of three dice to multiply together.

Challenge questions

- Can you invent a similar board game to practise division facts?
- Can you write all the factors of the numbers you cover?

Stand in line

> Stand in line is an activity for helping to introduce children to the term multiple.

Suitable for

KS1
KS2

Aims

- To develop multiplication facts up to 6 x 6.
- To develop and apply a mathematical strategy.

Players

- Small groups or pairs.

Resources

- 1–6 die
- Stand in line number grid
- Coloured counters

What to do

- Give each pair a copy of the number board shown here.

1	2	3	4	5	6
7	8	9	10	11	12
13	14	15	16	17	18
19	20	21	22	23	24
25	26	27	28	29	30
31	32	33	34	35	36

- Players roll a die to see who will start. Highest number rolled begins.
- Players take it in turns to roll the die and cover a multiple of their score. For example, with a 5 you could cover 5, 10, 15, 20, 25, 30 or 35.
- The winner is the first person to cover 4 multiples in a line.

Variations

- Change the game by practising multiples of 4, 5, 6, 7, 8 and 9 using a 4-9 die and numbers to match.
- Play as two players against two players.

Challenge questions

- Are there any numbers on the board that are never used?
- Can you invent your own game involving no redundant numbers?

Gimme five

Gimme five is a simple three in a row multiplication game with an element of chance.

Suitable for

KS1
KS2

Aims

- To develop and refine multiplication skills.
- Derive and recall multiplication facts up to 12 x 12.
- To work more flexibly with numbers.

Players

- This is a game for 2 players

Resources

- 2 dice
- Different coloured counters
- Number grid

What to do

- Organise children into pairs and give them a copy of the number grid shown here.

1	2	3	4	5
2	6	8	12	4
3	36	16	24	3
4	18	9	15	2
5	4	3	2	1

- Take turns to throw two 1-6 dice.
- If you get a five then you can place a counter on any number on the number board.
- If you don't roll a five, multiply the two numbers together. Put a counter on your answer. If the number is already covered then your turn is over.
- The winner is the first player to get 3 counters in a row.

Variations

- Use different numbered dice. For example, use two dice labelled 6–11. You will have to renumber the grid to take account of larger products.
- Make the grid larger and include more numbers.
- If you throw a double six then you have to remover all of your counters.
- If you throw a double one then you are allowed to remove two of your partner's counters.

Challenge questions

- Is the game fair? How much strategy does the game involve? Is the game based on luck?
- Can you make the game more demanding? For example, if you throw a double four then you have to say the four times table backwards.

At sixes and sevens

At sixes and sevens is an effective multiplication game for learning the multiples of 6 and 7.

Suitable for

KS1
KS2

Aims

- To develop and refine multiplication skills.
- Derive and recall multiplication facts up to 12 x 12.
- To work more flexibly with numbers.

Players

- This is a game for 2 players

Resources

- 2 dice labelled 4–9
- Different coloured counters
- At sixes and sevens number grid

What to do

- Organise players into pairs and give out the 'At sixes and sevens' number grid shown here.

24	63	36	42	28
35	35	54	30	49
56	48	42	63	30
24	28	42	49	56
48	36	30	24	24

- Players have a die each.
- Player A rolls the die and multiples their score by 6 and covers an answer on the board.
- Player B rolls the die and multiplies their score by 7 and covers an answer on the board.
- The aim of the game is to get three counters in a straight line on the number board.

Variations

- This game can be played for any multiplication table. Try the game for 3 and 4, 7 and 8, 8 and 9 etc. remembering to generate new numbers for the number board.
- The winner is the player to cover the most numbers.

Challenge questions

- If you play three in a row to win, can you multiply the numbers you have covered together?
- Can you invent your own version of this game for 9 and 12?

A bit dicey

A bit dicey is an enjoyable multiplication game that helps children to practise and improve their multiplication skills.

Suitable for

KS1
KS2

Aims

- To develop and refine multiplication skills.
- Derive and recall multiplication facts up to 12 x 12.
- To work more flexibly with numbers.

Players

- This is a game for 2 or 3 players

Resources

- Two 1–6 dice
- One 6–11 die
- Number grid
- Coloured counters

What to do

- Children team up with a maths buddy.
- Give children a copy of the number grid, one between two.
- Take turns to throw the three dice.
- The two 1–6 dice are added together and then multiplied by the 6–11 die.
- If the result matches a number on the number grid then cover that number with a coloured counter.

- Keep a record of how you made the number each time for someone else to check.
- The winner is the first player to have four counters in any one row (they do not have to be joined).

72	42	90	24	33	132	35
14	36	32	40	44	12	48
55	7	54	108	70	56	120
18	63	45	88	27	9	60
96	8	72	21	49	50	11
80	20	100	16	64	99	18
48	22	132	6	84	10	28

Variations

- The number grid could be made bigger or smaller depending on the ability of the children.
- The numbers could be congregated differently with more repeats of particular numbers. For example, you might decide to include 42 six times and 64 only once.
- Rather than four in a row you could say four numbers in any column – again, they don't have to be joined.
- Play continues until both players have covered eight squares and then players add up the numbers under the counters to get a total score. The player with the most points is the winner.

Challenge question

- Can you think about using a die in another way? For example, could you use four 1–6 dice – what changes would you make to the rules and what changes would you need to make to the number grid?

I spy

> I spy is a fast 'think on your feet' multiplication game to help children with their mental agility when finding products.

Suitable for

KS1
KS2

Aims

- To develop and refine multiplication skills.
- Derive and recall multiplication facts up to 12 x 12.
- To work more flexibly with numbers.

Players

- This is a game for 3 players

Resources

- A pack of playing cards or a couple of sets of 0–12 digit cards

What to do

- Shuffle a pack of 52 playing cards, leaving in all picture cards and jokers.
- Organise children into threes. One player is the spy and the other two compete against each other.
- Place the playing cards face up in 7 rows and 7 columns. Cards left over place to one side.
- One player acts as the spy by calling out products. For example, 'I spy with my maths eye 24.'
- The other two players search for two numbers that make the number called.

- The numbers have to be next to each other either horizontally, vertically or diagonally.
- Players put up their hands if they find two numbers that make the product called, point to them and take the cards from the 8 x 8 grid if everyone agrees that the numbers have been multiplied together correctly.
- A joker can stand for any number and picture cards equal 10. An ace makes 1 or 11.
- Play continues like this and as more cards are removed, the spy moves the remaining cards closer together so there are no gaps.
- The winner is the player with the most cards at the end of the game.
- Play a new game and take turns being the maths spy who calls out the products.

Variations

- Use a smaller grid size.
- This could be played as a game of I spy division where the spy calls out a division sum, 'I spy with my maths eye 7.' This game would require number digit cards larger than those used for the multiplication game.
- Rather than have a rule where numbers have to be next to each other players can point to numbers anywhere on the grid and take them if they multiply together to make the product called.
- You could call out two products at a time for players to find.

Challenge questions

- Can you think of different ways of saying the products? For example, 'I spy with my maths eye 6 squared.'
- Can you think of a way of scoring other than collecting the most cards? For example, adding up the scores printed on the cards.

Trebles

Trebles is a simple but clever multiplication game that children create themselves.

Suitable for

KS1
KS2

Aims

- To develop and refine multiplication skills.
- To work more flexibly with numbers.

Players

- This is a game for 2 players

Resources

- Paper and pencils (or whiteboards and pens)
- 6 x 6 number grid
- Coloured counters
- Die

What to do

- Give children a 6 x 6 empty grid or ask them to draw a grid themselves.
- Children team up with a maths buddy ready to play.
- Tell children to take turns rolling a die.
- Treble the number rolled and write the number rolled in any square on the grid.
- Continue taking turns rolling the die and filling the grid with trebled numbers until the grid is full.
- Now take turns to roll the die again. Treble your answer and place a coloured counter on the number you have made.
- The winner is the first player to get four in a row, vertically, horizontally or diagonally.

Variations

- Instead of trebles you could make this doubles or quadruples or multiply by any number you want to practise.
- The grid can be made as big or as small as you want depending on the age group and ability level of the children.
- Rather than four in a row, you could say the first player to make an L-shape.
- Award bonus points for particular squares. For example, if you cover a square in any of the corners, then have another go.

Challenge questions

- Is this game fair? Is there a fair way of starting other than rolling a die or tossing a coin?
- How could you vary the rules? Could you use two dice?
- Can you think of a points system for this game rather than four in a row?

How many?

How many? is a fun activity that encourages children to practise their multiplication skills using unusual questions.

Suitable for

KS1
KS2

Aims

- To multiply large numbers.
- To work more confidently with numbers.
- To work cooperatively together.

Players

- Small groups or pairs

Resources

- Paper and pencils (or whiteboards and pens)

What to do

- Ask children to think about how many 'eyes' there are in the class. Work this out together. Now ask children to work out how many fingers and toes there are in the class. Calculate the answer together.
- Now encourage children to think about other animals apart from themselves. For example, if there are 239 chickens how many wings is that?
- Now show children the following list and ask them to work out the solution to each one:

193 octopuses – how many arms?
226 spiders – how many legs?
378 ladybirds – how many legs?
949 dragonflies – how many wings?
898 scorpions – how many legs?
1,063 flies – how many legs?

- Go through the answers together and tell children that a ladybird has 6 legs, a dragonfly has 4 wings, and a scorpion has 8 legs. Do they need to recalculate their answers?
- Ask children to invent their own number problems like this based on other animals.

Variations

- Increase or decrease the number of animals as appropriate.
- Join some problems together. For example, 29 chickens, 39 dragonflies and 115 seagulls – how many wings?
- Think about some number prefixes and ask children questions based on these. For example, how many legs do 3,786 tripods have? How many babies would 4,599 sets of triplets be? How many sets of quadruplets would 1,800 be?

Challenge questions

- Are there any creatures with more than 8 legs?
- How many number prefixes do you know? What do they mean? E.g. pentathlon, heptathlon, decathlon.
- Read the following rhyme and then work out how many people and animals were going to St Ives.

As I was going to St Ives,
I met a man with seven wives,
Every wife had seven sacks,
Every sack had seven cats,
Every cat had seven kits.

Bingo bango!

Bingo bango! is an exciting activity for helping children to multiply and divide a range of numbers by 1, 10, 100 and 1,000.

Suitable for

KS1
KS2

Aims

- To multiply and divide whole and decimal numbers.
- To work more confidently with numbers.

Players

- Small groups or pairs

Resources

- 1–6 die
- Die covered as follows: x1, x10, x100, x1,000, ÷10, ÷100
- Bingo bango! number grid
- Coloured counters

What to do

- Give children a copy each of the Bingo bango! number grid shown here and two dice.
- Take turns to roll the dice and then do the multiplication or division made. For example, if you threw a 5 and ÷100 then this would make 0.05.
- Cover the answer you make with one of your counters.
- The player to get one column completed is the winner.

1	10	100	1000	0.1	0.01
2	20	200	2000	0.2	0.02
3	30	300	3000	0.3	0.03
4	40	400	4000	0.4	0.04
5	50	500	5000	0.5	0.05
6	60	600	6000	0.6	0.06

Variations

- Change one of the die so that it is labelled x1, x10, x10, x100, x100, x1000.
- The 1–6 die could be labelled from 4 to 9 and the Bingo bango! grid changed to represent new values as appropriate.
- Change the way the game is won. For example, two numbers covered in all columns.

Challenge questions

- Would the game be fair if it was agreed that you could only start playing once a double had been thrown?
- Could you use a different shaped die? What values would you include on a die with 10 faces?

Multi-key

> Multi-key is a calculator multiplication game to help children multiply single-digit and 2-digit numbers together.

Suitable for

KS2

Aims

- To multiply single-digit and 2-digit numbers together.
- To work more confidently with numbers using a calculator.

Players

- An activity for two players

Resources

- Calculators
- Multi-key grid
- Coloured counters

What to do

- Give children a copy of the Multi-key number grid shown here.
- Now write the following numbers on the board: 3, 7, 11, 21, 19, 29, 53, 61.
- Tell children that they have to pick two numbers from the list and multiply them together using their calculator.
- If they can make a number on the grid then they cover that number with a counter.
- The first player to get 4 in a row is the winner.

779	451	1537	209	57	1769
21	203	551	319	63	2173
3233	33	861	671	1281	371
2501	287	427	609	583	133
77	231	123	1159	183	1113
87	159	1189	1007	399	147

Variations

- Include new numbers to add to the list. Work out their product combinations and then include a new row and column on the grid.
- Instead of four in a row play according to a time limit and the player with the most counters on the grid is the winner.

Challenge questions

- Are there any number combinations not represented on the grid?
- If a player cannot make a number, what rule could you invent apart from missing

Chapter 5
Division

Digital roots

Digital roots is an activity to help children improve their division, reasoning and explanation skills.

Suitable for

KS2

Aims

- To divide a range of 2-digit numbers by a 1-digit number.
- Refine pencil and paper methods.

Players

- This is an activity for 2 players

Resources

- Two sets of 1–9 digit cards
- Paper and pencils
- Calculator

What to do

- Give pair a set of 1–9 digit cards.
- Players shuffle the cards and then take two to make a 2-digit number. For example, 59.
- Players then find the digital root of this number. For example, $5 + 9 = 14, 1 + 4 = 5$.
- When the digital root has been found, players then divide 59 by this number. So, $59 \div 5 = 11$ remainder 4 or remainder $\frac{4}{5}$.
- Play continues like this and players keep a running total of their remainders.
- The first player to reach 30 or more is the winner.

Variations

- Play with 3-digit numbers, 4-digit or 5-digit numbers instead.
- If the digital root is 1 then it is your turn.

Challenge questions

- Is there a connection between the number made and its digital root? For example, $29 = 2 + 9 = 11$ and $1 + 1 = 2$. Is the digital root always the tens digit?
- Can you investigate different numbers and make some statements about them for another group to investigate? For example, the digital roots of odd numbers under 30 are either 1, 2 or 3.

On average

On average is an activity to help children find the mean average of a set of data.

Suitable for

KS2

Aims

- To solve problems using the mean, mode, median and range.
- Refine pencil and paper methods.

Players

- This is an activity for 2 players

Resources

- Two sets of 1–9 digit cards
- 1–6 die
- Paper and pencils
- Calculator

What to do

- Give each pair a set of digit cards.
- Players shuffle the cards and place them in a pile on the table.
- Players then take it in turns to take six cards.
- The cards are then added together and divided by 6 to find the average.
- The answer is checked on a calculator.
- The average is then counted as the score.
- Cards taken are put to one side and shuffled.
- The player with the most points after an agreed number of turns is the winner.

Variations

- You can take fewer cards or more cards.
- Instead of 0–9 cards, include 2-digit cards.
- You could take five cards and then roll a 4–9 die three times and add the total together.

Challenge question

- Can you work out the range? the mode? the median?

Estimation time

> Estimation time is an activity to help children understand more about number properties including the numbers they are divisible by.

Suitable for

KS2

Aims

- To recognise which numbers are divisible by 2, 3, 4, 5 and 6.
- Refine pencil-and-paper methods.

Players

- This is a game for 2–4 players

Resources

- Estimation grid
- 1–6 die
- Coloured counters
- Paper and pencils
- Calculator

What to do

- Give players a copy of the grid shown here.
- Each player rolls a die three times. The first roll gives the unit digit, the second roll gives the tens digit and the third roll gives the hundreds digit. For example, 416.
- The die is rolled again, e.g. 5.
- Each player now has to estimate how many times 5 will go into 416.
- Players record their estimate.

Number made	Die number	Player 1	Player 2	Player 3	Player 4	Actual division

- The sum is then worked out on a calculator and rounded up or down to give a whole number answer.
- The closest estimate scores 4 points.
- An estimate that is correct scores 12 points.
- Play this game six more times to find the overall winner.

Number made	Die number	Player 1	Player 2	Player 3	Player 4	Actual division
416	5	33	56	60	70	416/5 = 83.2

Variations

- Roll to make a 2-digit number rather than a 3-digit number.
- Roll to make a 4-digit number.
- The first player to make 25 points is the winner.
- Players can play in pairs against each other.

Challenge question

- Can you work out the quotients without a calculator?

Snake division

Snake division is an activity to help children understand more about number properties including the numbers they are divisible by.

Suitable for

KS1
KS2

Aims

- To recognise which numbers are divisible by 2, 3, 4, 5 and 6.
- Refine pencil and paper methods.

Players

- This is a game for two players

Resources

- Snake number grid
- 1–6 die
- Coloured counters
- Paper and pencils

What to do

- Give everyone a copy of a number snake as shown.

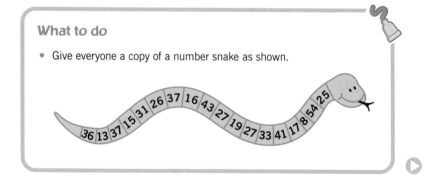

- Players get into pairs and roll the die. The highest number starts.
- Start on the tail of the snake. Roll the die and move your counter that number of spaces forward.
- Now divide the number you land on by the number on the die. For example, if you throw a 3 and then land on 35, you divide 37 by 3 then you get 12 remainder 1. One point would be scored because this was the remainder.
- Play continues up to the head of the snake and back down to the tail.
- The player with the most points (totalling all the remainders) is the winner.

Variations

- You can use a different die (4–9).
- Include 2 snakes each containing a different set of numbers so each player has their own snake.
- Play to reach the head of the snake rather than there and back again.
- Convert the remainders into fractions and add the fractions together.
- If you throw two 6s in succession then take off all your points.

Challenge questions

- Can you invent a game like this but as a race track instead of a snake? What rules would you change/add?
- How can the game be improved? For example, could you invent a version of snakes and ladders where the numbers used are those from 1–100 rather than those printed on the snake? Could you play it whereby you go down a ladder and up an adder (the snake)?

What am I?

What am I? is an activity to help children understand more about number properties including the numbers they are divisible by.

Suitable for

KS1
KS2

Aims

- To recognise which numbers are divisible by 2, 4 and 5.
- Refine pencil-and-paper methods.

Players

- This is a game for two players

Resources

- What am I? grid
- Coloured pencils/felts
- Paper and pencils

What to do

- Give everyone a copy of the What am I? number grid shown here.

43	42	25	39
30	48	33	38
32	15	40	17
29	21	36	20
10	18	22	35

- Ask children to work together to double-check their understanding. Circle all the numbers which are divisible by 4 in green. Circle all the numbers divisible by 5 in red and circle all the numbers divisible by 2 in blue.
- Remind children that some numbers may be circled more than once.
- Now challenge children to complete the following number sentences: all numbers divisible by 4 are also divisible by_____, a number divisible by 2 and 5 is also divisible by_____, a number divisible by 2,4 and 5 is also divisible by_____.

Variations

- You can invent different grids for different table groups containing different numbers and then compare and contrast answers.
- Try this activity for other numbers. For example, try circling numbers which are divisible by 3, 6 and 9.

Challenge questions

- Can you write down other numbers which are also divisible by 2,4 and 5?
- Can you find all the factors of the numbers you have circled?
- Can you add up all the numbers in a row and then see whether the total divides by 2, 4 and 5? Do the same for the column totals and diagonals as well.

Fishing line

Fishing line is a fun activity to help children improve their division skills.

Suitable for

KS1
KS2

Aims

- To divide 1-digit and 2-digit numbers by a 1-digit number.
- Refine pencil and paper methods.

Players

- This is a game for two players

Resources

- Fishing line number board
- A 1–6 die
- Coloured counters
- Paper and pencils

What to do

- Organise children into pairs and give them a copy of the Fishing line number grid shown on page 151.
- Explain to players that the aim of the game is to cover four numbers on the board.
  To do this players roll a die and then select a number on the grid that will divide exactly. For example, if you threw a 4 then 16 could be covered because this divides four times exactly.

- Remind children that remainders are not allowed and that a number has to be exactly divisible.
- If a player throws a 1 then they miss a go.

45	25	18	44	24	5
20	12	8	50	14	35
36	22	45	42	10	34
38	60	52	40	28	18
46	55	25	16	15	14

Variations

- You can include some higher numbers or increase the grid size.
- Score the number that you cover. This would allow remainders to be played. For example, if you rolled a 3 and you selected 22, then this would be 7 remainder 1. The remainder would then be subtracted from 22 giving a score of 21. It could be a better strategy to aim for numbers with a remainder if the number is a high number.
- Play where the winner is the player to get a counter in each column.

Challenge question

- Can you vary the game to provide an element of luck? For example, rather than choose any number on the board, the die is rolled twice. Once to say which number column you have to select a number from and once more to show what number you will use to divide by.

Leftovers

Leftovers is an enjoyable activity to help children learn more about remainders.

Suitable for

KS1
KS2

Aims

- To divide 2-digit numbers by a 1-digit number.
- Refine pencil and paper methods.

Players

- This is a game for individual players or two players

Resources

- Two sets of 3–9 digit cards
- A 1–6 die
- Paper and pencils

What to do

- Organise children into pairs. This game could be played independently too.
- Shuffle together a set of 3–9 digit cards and place them face down on the table.
- Players take it in turns to take two cards.
- The cards are then combined to make two 2-digit numbers. For example, 2 and 4 could make 24 and 42.
- Roll the die. If a 1 is rolled then miss your go.

- Divide the numbers by the number rolled. If there is a remainder then score that number of points. For example, if you rolled a 3 then no points would be scored. If you rolled a 5 the 6 points would be scored because 24 ÷ 5 = 4 remainder 4 and 42 ÷ 5 = 8 remainder 2.
- The winner is the first player to score 30 or more.

Variations

- You can play this game with counters instead of points and give each counter a monetary value. For example, each counter is worth 20p.
- Play the game with a different die, e.g. 4–9.
- Make just one 2-digit number rather than 2. For example, make the smallest number or the largest number.
- Take it in turns to make a 3-digit number, a 4-digit number, etc.
- If you throw a one, then score 6 points.

Challenge questions

- Can you express the remainders as a fraction? For example, 24 ÷ 5 = 4 and 4/5
- Can you invent a similar game involving more than one die?

Hexadivision

Hexadivision is a simple activity to help children learn various divisibility tests.

Suitable for

KS1
KS2

Aim

- Use tests of divisibility to estimate and check answers.

Players

- This is a game for 2 players

Resources

- Two sets of 0–9 digit cards
- Paper and pencils
- Hexagadivision shape
- Calculator

What to do

- Organise children into pairs and give them a copy of a drawing of a hexagon, with the following in each vertex: ÷3, ÷4, ÷6, ÷7, ÷8, ÷9, and three empty squares in the middle of the hexagon.
- Players take three cards from a well-shuffled pack of digit cards and place them in the middle of the hexagon.
- Both players then have to rearrange the digits so that they are divisible by each number shown. This could be calculated using a pencil and paper or calculator or both.

- Points are awarded according to the division made. For example, if the digits 3, 4 and 2 were chosen then 6 would divide into this scoring 57 points (342 ÷ 6 = 57) and 38 points for 342 ÷ 9 = 38. This would give a total of 57 and 38 = 95.
- The player with the most points after six rounds is the winner.

Variations

- You can alter the shape perhaps to a square, a pentagon, a heptagon or octagon. The numbers in each corner of the shapes chosen can then be altered accordingly.
- Points could be scored differently. Instead of looking for numbers that are exactly divisible by the numbers in each corner, work out what the quotients are and round to the nearest whole.
- To help children, list divisibility tests on the board or print them off as a helpline for children to refer to. For example,

  2 = the last digit is even (0, 2, 4, 6, or 8).
  3 = the sum of the digits is divisible by 3.
  4 = the last two digits divisible by 4.
  5 = the last digit is 0 or 5.
  6 = it is divisible by 2 and by 3.
  7 = subtract 2 times the last digit from the rest.
  8 = last 3 digits divisible by 8.
  9 = sum of digits divisible by 9.

Challenge questions

- Can you make a poster of the divisibility tests to help other children?
- Can you find the divisibility tests for 10, 11 and 12?

Complete convert

Complete convert is an activity to help children turn fractions into decimals.

Suitable for

KS2

Aims

- Understand percentage as the number of parts in every 100 and express tenths and hundredths as percentages.
- Order a set of fractions by converting them to decimals.

Players

- This is a game for 2 players

Resources

- 2 dice
- Complete convert division grid
- Coloured counters
- Calculators

What to do

- Organise children into pairs and give them a copy of the Complete convert division grid shown here.
- Players take it in turn to select a fraction on the board and convert it into a decimal number.
- Players check each other's decimal conversion using a calculator.
- If a decimal number can be made accurately then a counter is placed on the fraction square. For example, if someone chose $\frac{3}{5}$ and said 0.6, then a counter could be placed on $\frac{3}{5}$.
- The winner is the first player to have four counters in a line.

$\frac{1}{8}$	$\frac{10}{30}$	$\frac{19}{50}$	$\frac{1}{1000}$	$\frac{7}{1000}$	$\frac{8}{10}$
$\frac{3}{15}$	$\frac{1}{3}$	$\frac{27}{100}$	$\frac{3}{5}$	$\frac{9}{10}$	$\frac{20}{30}$
$\frac{1}{100}$	$\frac{4}{8}$	$\frac{3}{4}$	$\frac{33}{50}$	$\frac{2}{8}$	$\frac{27}{50}$
$\frac{2}{1000}$	$\frac{9}{50}$	$\frac{2}{4}$	$\frac{41}{50}$	$\frac{15}{50}$	$\frac{1}{10}$
$\frac{17}{25}$	$\frac{12}{25}$	$\frac{5}{1000}$	$\frac{10}{80}$	$\frac{3}{100}$	$\frac{1}{5}$
$\frac{7}{100}$	$\frac{23}{25}$	$\frac{6}{8}$	$\frac{1}{4}$	$\frac{15}{1000}$	$\frac{9}{1000}$
$\frac{4}{5}$	$\frac{2}{3}$	$\frac{7}{10}$	$\frac{2}{5}$	$\frac{127}{1000}$	$\frac{2}{10}$

Variations

- You can tailor the level of difficulty and select different fractions to go on the board.
- Instead of four in a line, players can win by getting two lines of three anywhere on the board.

Challenge questions

- Can you make the decimal version of this game where the squares are filled with decimals and players have to turn them into fractions?
- Can you order the numbers you have covered on a decimal number line?

Division squares

> Division squares is an activity to help children derive and recall multiplication facts up to 10 x 10 and corresponding division facts.

Suitable for

KS2

Aims

- To derive and recall multiplication facts up to 10 x 10.
- To derive and recall division facts and multiples of numbers to 10 up to the tenth multiple.

Players

- This is a game for 2 players

Resources

- 2 dice
- Division grids 1 and 2

What to do

- Players get into pairs and roll a die each. Division board 1 is given to the player with the highest number and division board 2 to the player with the lowest number.

Division board 1

4	8	3
5	1	7
2	6	9

Division board 2

7	2	8
1	3	5
4	6	9

- Players take it in turns to throw both dice to make a 2-digit number. For example, 14.
- Place a counter on any number that will go into the number you have thrown. For example, 2 will go into 14 so you can place a counter on number 2.
- The winner is the first player to get three in a row.
- Play the best of five games to find the overall winner.

Variations

- You could double the boards in size so that the game is played with 18 numbers from 1 to 9 on each board. To win players have to get four or five in a row.
- You could use a bigger style board of numbers between two rather than one board each.
- You could use one 1–6 die and one 4–9 die.
- The numbers on the board could be changed to include bigger divisors.

Challenge questions

- Why do games have to be played as the best out of 3? 5? 7? or any other odd number?
- Can you think of a way of playing this game with three dice? For example, roll three dice and make a 2-digit number out of just two of them.
- Can the game be played whereby one player can take another player's counter?
- For example, if you throw a double you can remove an opponent's counter?

A matter of factor

A matter of factor is an activity to help children recognise factors of numbers.

Suitable for

KS1
KS2

Aims

- To recognise a pair of factors of a number.
- To recognise that any number has itself and 1 as factors.
- To list the factors of a number.

Players

- This is a game for 2 players

Resources

- 1–9 digit cards

What to do

- Children get into pairs and shuffle a set of 1–9 digit cards.
- Players then take two cards each and place them face up on the table.
- Explain to children that the aim of the activity is to use the four digits to make 2-digit numbers so that the numbers 2–9 can be divided into them exactly. For example, if the digits drawn out of the pile of 1–9 cards are 2, 6, 3 and 5 then pairs have to make numbers that 2 will go into (26), 3 will go into (36), 4 will go into (36) and so on. This could be set out as a table as follows:

Digits selected: 2 6 3 5

Factor	Number made	Points scored
2 is a factor of	26	13
3 is a factor of		
4 is a factor of		
5 is a factor of		
6 is a factor of		
7 is a factor of		
8 is a factor of		
9 is a factor of		

- Score points according to the number made divided by the factor. For example, 2 is a factor of 26 would equal 13 points because $26 \div 2 = 13$.
- Put the cards back into the pack, shuffle and play the game again to see how many points can be scored.

Variations

- Find all the factors of the numbers made.
- Identify which numbers in your list have the most factors.
- Restrict the number of times a digit can be used. For example, after the digit cards have been selected, players can only use a digit up to four times.
- Play this activity where you make 3-digit numbers or 5-digit numbers.

Challenge questions

- Why do square numbers have an odd number of factors?
- Can you find a set of four digits that will fit into every factor sentence?

Remains of the day

Remains of the day is an enjoyable board game for helping children practise their division skills and understand remainders.

Suitable for

KS1
KS2

Aims

- To divide whole numbers.
- To derive and recall multiplication facts and related division facts.

Players

- A game for two players

Resources

- Paper and pencils (or whiteboards and pens).
- A number board
- A die
- Coloured counters

What to do

- Organise players into maths buddies and give them a copy of the number grid shown here.
- Players take it in turns to roll the die and the lowest number starts.
- Roll the die again. This is your remainder.
- Now divide 2, 3, 4, 5, 6 or 7 into one of the numbers on the board to get the remainder shown on the die. For example if you threw a 2 you need to find a number with a remainder of 2. You could divided 14 by 6 to get a remainder of 2.

- Put a counter on the number used on the board, e.g. 14, as in the example above.
- If you cannot make a number on the board then it is the other player's go.
- The winner is the player with the most counters on the board after ten turns each.

3	4	5	6	7	8
9	10	11	12	13	14
15	16	17	18	19	20
21	22	23	24	25	26
27	28	29	30	31	32
33	34	35	36	37	38

Variations

- The board size could be increased to include more numbers.
- You could play with four number boards with random numbers printed on each. The idea of the game would be to get three counters on each board to win the game.
- You could play with three dice. One die would be thrown as in the example above in order to get the remainder. The other two dice could be thrown as a bonus throw whereby if a double was thrown, then that player could remove an opponent's counter.

Challenge questions

- Can you express each of the remainders as fractions? For example, $18 \div$ by 5 would make $3\frac{3}{5}$.
- Can you play the game where the winner is the player who places three counters on the board where the remainder is always a remainder of 4?
- Do the numbers on the board have to be placed consecutively? Does it make a difference if the numbers 3–38 are placed randomly?

Divide and conquer

Divide and conquer is a great game for helping children practise their division skills.

Suitable for

KS1
KS2

Aims

- To divide whole numbers.
- To derive and recall multiplication facts and related division facts.

Players

- A game for two players

Resources

- Paper and pencils (or whiteboards and pens)
- Two division boards
- 2 dice
- Coloured counters

What to do

- Organise players into maths buddies and give each player a copy of one of the division boards shown on page 165.
- Players take turns to throw the dice in order to make a 2-digit number. For example, a six and a one could make 61 or 16.
- Players place a counter on a square whose number can be divided exactly into the 2-digit number made.
- The winner is the player who can make a block of four squares anywhere on the board.

Player A

3	9	6	4	1
5	2	2	5	8
4	6	7	3	7
9	9	8	1	3
5	8	7	2	6

Variations

- The size of the board could be made bigger or smaller as appropriate.
- Four dice could be thrown and two 2-digit numbers made at the same time.
- Throw four dice but discard one pair after you have made a 2-digit number out of the four.
- Instead of the winner making a block of four to win, adapt the rules so that it is three in a row, four in a row, top horizontal line, bottom horizontal line, four corners and the centre, etc.
- Instead of four in a row, etc. the aim of the game could be to cover as many squares as possible in a timed game of five minutes and the numbers covered equal the points scored. The winner is the player with the most squares covered or the most points scored.

Challenge questions

- Are the two boards fair? Look at the numbers and decide whether one board has more chance than the other.
- How could you adapt the layout of numbers written on the division boards? Does it matter that the numbers are placed randomly in the boxes?
- Can you think of a reward square? For example, if you included only one number 7 on your board perhaps this could mean an extra go.

Deci·divide

Deci-divide is an enjoyable game for helping children practise their division skills using a calculator to make decimal numbers.

Suitable for

KS1
KS2

Aims

- Use understanding of place value to divide whole numbers and decimals.
- To derive and recall multiplication facts and related division facts.
- Use a calculator to solve problems.

Players

- A game for two players

Resources

- Paper and pencils (or whiteboards and pens)
- Decimal division board
- Coloured counters

What to do

- Organise players into pairs and give them a copy of the Deci-divide grid shown here.
- Ask children to choose two numbers between 1 and 10 and divide one number by the other using a calculator.
- If the quotient made is a decimal number on the board then cover that number with a counter. If not, wait until your next go to try again.
- The winner is the first player to place four counters in a row in any direction.

2.0	0.75	0.8	7.0	0.6
3.5	1.25	0.25	0.9	1.125
0.2	0.7	2.5	0.675	1.5
5.0	1.125	0.625	3.0	0.1
0.3	0.4	0.5	4.5	4.0

Variations

- Rather than numbers from 1–10, you could include numbers from 1–20. This would mean working out the other decimal combinations and representing them on a bigger board.
- Instead of four in a row, four in a block wins.
- The player with the most counters on the board wins.
- Players add up the decimal numbers they cover and the first to reach over 10 is the winner.

Challenge questions

- Can you play this game without using a calculator?
- Can you round each number to the nearest tenth?
- Can you add each diagonal, row and column?

Chapter 6
Logical reasoning

Who's who?

Who's who? involves children working with a small set of clues in order to complete a table of results.

Suitable for

KS1
KS2

Aims

- Describe ways of solving puzzles and problems, explaining choices and decisions orally or using pictures.
- Explain reasoning using diagrams, graphs and text.
- To plan and pursue an enquiry.
- Explore patterns, properties and relationships.

Players

- This is an activity suitable for small maths groups.

Resources

- Pencil and paper

What to do

- Show children the table shown here.

	11	7	6	8	10
Bianca					
Mia					
Dwight					
Luke					
Eddie					

- Explain to children that the challenge is to work out how old each child is. Explain that you have some clues to help them.
- Begin with the first clue: 'Eddie is three years younger than Mia.'
- Talk about this statement and show children how the table can be partially filled in using this clue. Say that you will use Y for Yes and N for No and fill in the table as follows:

	11	7	6	8	10
Bianca					
Mia		N	N	N	
Dwight					
Luke					
Eddie	N		N		N

- Now provide children with the second clue – 'Bianca is two years younger than Dwight.' Use this information to fill in more of the table together as follows:

	11	7	6	8	10
Bianca	N	N			N
Mia		N	N	N	
Dwight	N	N	N		
Luke					
Eddie	N		N		N

- Now share the last clue and complete the table: 'Bianca is five years younger than Luke.'

	11	7	6	8	10
Bianca	N	N	Y	N	N
Mia	N	N	N	N	Y
Dwight	N	N	N	Y	N
Luke	Y	N	N	N	N
Eddie	N	Y	N	N	N

Variations

- Place the ages in order on top of the table.
- Use fewer children in the problem. For example:

	6	7	8	9
Stephi				
Joss				
Vikram				
Daniel				

Joss is three years older than Stephi.
Vikram is one year younger than Daniel.
Vikram is one year older than Stephi.

Solution:
Joss is three years older than Stephi.

	6	7	8	9
Stephi	Y	N	N	N
Joss	N	N	N	Y
Vikram	N			N
Daniel	N			N

Vikram is one year younger than Daniel.

	6	7	8	9
Stephi	Y	N	N	N
Joss	N	N	N	Y
Vikram	N			N
Daniel	N			N

Vikram is one year older than Stephi.

	6	7	8	9
Stephi	Y	N	N	N
Joss	N	N	N	Y
Vikram	N	Y	N	N
Daniel	N	N	Y	N

Challenge questions

- Can you invent the clues for a problem involving six children shown in the grid below?

	6	10	11	12	13	14
Aidan						
Ripley						
Winston						
Katie						
Katherine						
Reid						

Bings and bangs

Bings and bangs is a number detective game involving code-breaking and mathematical reasoning.

Suitable for

KS1
KS2

Aims

- To identify a mystery number through deduction and a process of elimination.
- To work more confidently with numbers.

Players

- This game is best played in pairs

Resources

- Paper and pencils (or whiteboards and pens)

What to do

- Player A thinks of a 4-digit number, for example 1863, and writes it down. The digits all have to be different.
- Player B then guesses what this secret number might be by saying any 4-digit number, for example 8962.
- Player A reveals how close this guess is by saying how many bings and bangs have been scored. A bing means that the guess contains a correct digit but in the wrong position. A bang means that the guess contains a correct digit in the right position. So 8962 would be 1 bing and 1 bang.
- Player B uses this information to guess again with Player A revealing how many bings and bangs are scored.
- The game continues until Player B identifies four bangs.
- Players then swap over and change roles. The player who finds the secret number with the fewest guesses wins.

Variations

- Try playing with 5 or 6 digits instead of 4 (or fewer for younger or less confident learners) and work out the minimum number of moves needed to win.
- Create your own rules and version of the game, e.g. to include decimal numbers.

Challenge questions

- How much skill or luck is involved in the game?
- What is the smallest number of guesses you could use to win?
- How could the game be improved?

Ice·cream cone

Ice-cream cone is a problem that involves children looking at various clues in order to solve a problem step by step.

Suitable for

KS1
KS2

Aims

- Represent a puzzle or problem by identifying and recording the information or calculations needed to solve it; find possible solutions and confirm them in the context of the problem.
- Explain reasoning using diagrams, graphs and text; refine ways of recording using images and symbols.
- Explain reasoning and conclusions, using words, symbols or diagrams as appropriate.

Players

- This game is best played in pairs

Resources

- Paper and pencils (or whiteboards and pens)

What to do

- Introduce the problem to children as follows: I have an ice-cream cone with five scoops of ice cream on top. Each scoop is a different flavour of ice cream. The five flavours are blueberry, chocolate, strawberry, vanilla and bubblegum. You don't know what order my ice-cream flavours are from top to bottom.
- Ask children if there is any way of knowing what the flavours of ice cream are.

- Discuss that it would be impossible to know without some clues.
- Now provide the following clues to help children solve the problem:

  The bottom flavour has 10 letters.
  The vanilla scoop touches both the chocolate and blueberry scoop.
  Vanilla is below the chocolate scoop but above the bubblegum scoop.

- Now let children use their logic skills to work out the order of scoops by flavour.
- Share answers as a whole class and see who got the order correct as follows:

  From top to bottom, the flavours are:

  Chocolate
  Vanilla
  Blueberry
  Bubblegum
  Strawberry

Variations

- You could try this with different flavours and alter the clues accordingly.
- Add some more flavours to make it more challenging or one away.

Challenge questions

- How did you go about solving the problem?
- What was the most helpful clue?
- Could you solve the problem without the first clue?
- Can you make this problem more difficult?

Shoe size

Shoe size is a tricky problem that challenges children to work out the shoe sizes of five friends using different pieces of information and putting the clues together like a jigsaw.

Suitable for

KS1
KS2

Aims

- Represent a puzzle or problem by identifying and recording the information or calculations needed to solve it; find possible solutions and confirm them in the context of the problem.
- Explain reasoning using diagrams, graphs, and text; refine ways of recording using images and symbols.
- Explain reasoning and conclusions, using words, symbols or diagrams as appropriate.

Players

- This game is best played in pairs

Resources

- Paper and pencils (or whiteboards and pens)

What to do

- Introduce the problem to the class as follows: five friends leave their shoes in the hallway. They all have the same make of shoe but in a different size. The shoes are size 2, 3, 4, 5 and 6.
- Now read the following three clues to children and write them on the board:

Tanzina knows hers are the smallest shoes.

Kim thinks her shoes are bigger than Christian's but smaller than Daisy's.

Brandon knows his are the largest.

- Ask children to work together to solve the problem using the clues they have been given.
- Talk together about the most sensible way to solve the problem, i.e. by drawing a table.
- Let children decide on the table headings themselves and how best to complete it before sharing ideas from each group.
- Draw a table on the board as follows and then complete it step by step together explaining how to tick and cross each row/column.

	2	3	4	5	6
Tanzina	✓	X	X	X	X
Kim	X	X	✓	X	X
Christian	X	✓	X	X	X
Daisy	X	X	X	✓	X
Brandon	X	X	X	X	✓

Variations

- You could invent a similar problem but only have three or four children.
- Include more children and more shoe sizes.
- Personalise the names for the children in your class.
- Include some random clues that are superfluous to solving the problem. For example, 'Christian's shoes cost £39.99.'

Challenge questions

- How did drawing a table help with solving the problem?
- Could you have solved the problem without drawing a table?
- Has solving this problem given you a strategy for solving further problems?

Whose number?

> **Whose number?** challenges children to work out numbers belonging to four friends using logical reasoning and a process of elimination.

Suitable for

KS1
KS2

Aims

- Describe ways of solving puzzles and problems, explaining choices and decisions orally or using pictures.
- Explain reasoning using diagrams, graphs and text.
- To plan and pursue an enquiry.
- Explore patterns, properties and relationships.

Players

- This is an activity suitable for maths buddies

Resources

- Pencil and paper

What to do

- Introduce the problem as follows: Jenny, Jagdeep, Colin and Sadaf each picked a number from 20 to 99. One has 64, one has 43, one has 82, and one has 27.
- Now challenge children to work out what each person's number is according to the following clues:

The number whose tens digit is two and whose ones digit is seven is Colin's number.

Jagdeep's number comes before 65 and after 63.

Jenny's favourite number is not 43.

- Talk to children about the place value of each digit so that you can check they understand column value of digits.
- Children work in pairs and talk together about which number belongs to whom.
- Talk through the best way to record answers and decide on a strategy.
- Share solutions with each other and see who has the following:

  Jagdeep's number is 64, Sadaf's number is 43, Jenny's number is 82, Colin's number is 27.

- What was the easiest number to work out?
- Did it matter that there was no clue given for Sadaf? How did you work this number out?
- Could you have solved the problem with just two clues?

Variations

- You can increase the number of children to five and invent a new problem, e.g.

  Sheriyal, Anton, Tim, Kylie and Maisy each picked a number from 20 to 99. One has a number of 41, one has a number of 77, one has a number of 21, one has a number of 27, and one has a number of 38. Work out each person's number using the following clues:

  Kylie's number comes before 44 and after 38.
  The number whose tens digit is two and whose ones digit is one is Anton's number.
  Sheriyal's number comes before 42 and after 34.
  Tim's favourite number is not 27.

  Solution: Kylie's number is 41, Tim's number is 77, Anton's number is 21, Maisy's number is 27, Sheriyal's number is 38.

Challenge questions

- Can you invent a problem like the one above but with seven children? For example,

  John, Manny, Kris, Ali, Max, Dylan and Aran each picked a number from 20 to 99. One has a number of 62, one has a number of 91, one has a number of 58, one has a number of 30, one has a number of 31, one has a number of 66, and one has a number of 26.

  Can you work out what each person's number is?

  The number whose tens digit is two and whose ones digit is six is Manny's number.

  The number whose ones digit is one and whose tens digit is three is Ali's number.

  Kris's number comes before 60 and after 56.

  Max's favourite number is not 62.

  The number that Aran picked is between 27 and 33.

  John's number comes before 114 and after 68.

  Solution: Dylan's number is 62, John's number is 91, Kris's number is 58, Aran's number is 30, Ali's number is 31, Max's number is 66, and Manny's number is 26.

Recycle, recycle, recycle

Recycle, recycle, recycle challenges children to assemble various pieces of a jigsaw in order to solve a recycling problem.

Suitable for

KS1
KS2

Aims

- Describe ways of solving puzzles and problems, explaining choices and decisions orally or using pictures.
- Explain reasoning using diagrams, graphs and text.
- To plan and pursue an enquiry.
- Explore patterns, properties and relationships.

Players

- This is an activity suitable for small maths groups

Resources

- Pencil and paper

What to do

- Introduce the problem to children as follows:

  Alex, Corin, Ellie and Jazzy each recycled a different number of water bottles (18, 17, 20 and 16) as well as a different number of aluminium cans (103, 113, 131 and 122).
  Can you work out how many water bottles and aluminium cans each person recycled using the following clues?
  Corin recycled more than 16 water bottles.

If the number of water bottles Alex recycled was doubled she would have recycled 32 water bottles.

Alex recycled less than 131 cans.

Ellie recycled the most number of cans.

Ellie recyled a total of 151 water bottles and cans.

Jazzy recycled 86 more cans than the number of water bottles he recycled.

Alex recycled the least number of water bottles.

Corin and Ellie recyled a total of 291 water bottles and cans.

- For this problem, children can form groups of three to four as there is more information to handle.
- Encourage children to draw up a table if they think that would help them solve the problem, otherwise let them record their thinking in any way they want.
- When children have worked out the answers allow different groups the opportunity to verbalise their thinking and compare results.
- Share the solution with children and talk through the steps of the problem:

Alex recycled 16 water bottles and 113 cans; Ellie recycled 20 water bottles and 131 cans; Corin recycled 18 water bottles and 122 cans; and Jazzy recycled 17 water bottles and 103 cans.

Variations

- You can personalise the names of the children above to those in your class.
- Alter the recycled objects and the numbers involved.
- Invent a problem with fewer children.

Challenge questions

- Can you invent a problem with 5 children and 11 clues?
- Can you invent a problem with 6 children and 13 clues?
- Can you invent a problem with 7 children and 15 clues?

Homework

Homework invites children to think about how long four classmates take to complete their homework activities. Various clues are given for children to piece together in order to reach a logical conclusion and solve the problem.

Suitable for

KS1
KS2

Aims

- Describe ways of solving puzzles and problems, explaining choices and decisions orally or using pictures.
- Explain reasoning using diagrams, graphs and text.
- To plan and pursue an enquiry.
- Explore patterns, properties and relationships.

Players

- This is an activity suitable for small maths groups

Resources

- Pencil and paper

What to do

- Introduce the problem to children as follows:

  Ashley, Lialle, James and Junaid were each given some homework. They all took different times to finish it. One took 50 minutes, one took 70 minutes, one took 56 minutes, and one took 77 minutes to complete their homework.

How long did each person take to finish their homework?

Lialle started working 58 minutes after Junaid and finished 64 minutes after Jacob.

Junaid started working at 2.25. Ashley started working 15 minutes after Junaid and finished at 3.50.

- Now share the following clues with children and set maths buddies or small groups the task of finding out how long each person took to complete their homework:

James needed more time than Lialle to finish.

James started his homework at 6.48 p.m. and took a 35-minute break at 7.45 p.m. to eat his tea. He continued working after tea and finished the homework at 8.40 p.m.

Ashley needed more than an hour to finish.

Junaid started working 44 minutes after Ashley and finished twenty-four minutes after Ashley.

- Look through the clues carefully and decide together which clues point towards which pupil. Look at the clue which offers the most information. Is this the best starting point?
- Let children share with you their solutions. Write these on the board and then compare to the solution below:

Junaid took 50 minutes, Ashley took 70 minutes, Lialle took 56 minutes and James took 77 minutes

- Which group or groups managed to solve the problem?
- What difficulties did they experience? Were some clues more helpful than others? If you had to order the clues, which ones would go first?

Variation

- You can extend the Homework problem to include a greater number of pupils. For example, here is a problem involving five pupils:

Robbie, Ella, Justin, Jamille and Mitchell have all finished their homework in different times. One took 50 minutes, one took 84 minutes, one took 51 minutes, one took 87 minutes, and one took 55 minutes.

How long did each person take to finish their homework?

Mitchell started working 26 minutes after Jamille and finished 22 minutes after Jamille.

Mitchell needed more time than Robbie to finish.

Robbie needed less time than Justin to finish.

Jamille started working 58 minutes after Ella and finished 26 minutes after Ella.

Robbie started on his homework at 6.50 p.m. and then took a 37-minute break at 7.26 p.m. to watch TV. Robbie continued working after watching TV and finished his homework at 8.17 p.m.

Jamille needed less than an hour to finish.

Ella started working at 1.22. Justin started working 15 minutes after Ella and finished at 3.01.

Justin needed more time than Mitchell to finish.

Ella needed more than an hour to finish.

Justin needed more time than Jamille to finish

Robbie needed less than an hour to finish.

Solution: Robbie took 50 minutes, Justin took 84 minutes, Mitchell took 51 minutes, Ella took 87 minutes and Jamille took 55 minutes.

Challenge questions

- Can you invent a word problem with clues involving seven people?
- Could you solve this problem by drawing a table?
- What problem solving process did you follow?

How old?

How old? is an activity where children have to work out by logical reasoning the ages of five members of the same family. This involves a lot of mathematical detective step-by-step work.

Suitable for

KS1
KS2

Aims

- Describe ways of solving puzzles and problems, explaining choices and decisions orally or using pictures.
- Explain reasoning using diagrams, graphs and text.
- To plan and pursue an enquiry.
- Explore patterns, properties and relationships.

Players

- This is an activity suitable for small maths groups

Resources

- Pencil and paper

What to do

- Introduce the problem as follows:

  Five members of the same family go to the park together. They are Declan, Raeesah, Elif, Amreen and Spencer. They are all different ages. See if you can work out the age of each person using the clues below:

  Elif is 19 years younger than Raeesah.

  The sum of the ages of Elif and Raeesah is 113.

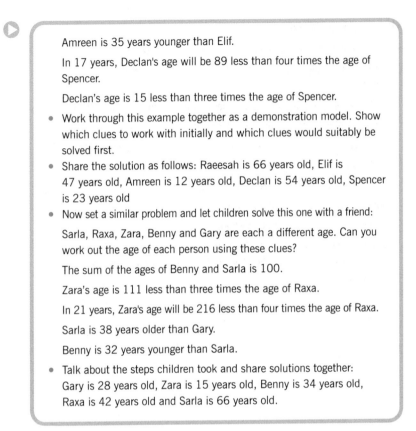

Amreen is 35 years younger than Elif.

In 17 years, Declan's age will be 89 less than four times the age of Spencer.

Declan's age is 15 less than three times the age of Spencer.

- Work through this example together as a demonstration model. Show which clues to work with initially and which clues would suitably be solved first.
- Share the solution as follows: Raeesah is 66 years old, Elif is 47 years old, Amreen is 12 years old, Declan is 54 years old, Spencer is 23 years old
- Now set a similar problem and let children solve this one with a friend:

  Sarla, Raxa, Zara, Benny and Gary are each a different age. Can you work out the age of each person using these clues?

  The sum of the ages of Benny and Sarla is 100.

  Zara's age is 111 less than three times the age of Raxa.

  In 21 years, Zara's age will be 216 less than four times the age of Raxa.

  Sarla is 38 years older than Gary.

  Benny is 32 years younger than Sarla.

- Talk about the steps children took and share solutions together: Gary is 28 years old, Zara is 15 years old, Benny is 34 years old, Raxa is 42 years old and Sarla is 66 years old.

Variations

- You can edit the number of people and increase them in order to make a more difficult problem.
- Personalise the names of the children to reflect your class.
- Change the ages.

Challenge question

- Can you invent a problem with seven people? For example,

  David, Billie, Jilly, Joe, Nishen, Zak and Jas are each a different age. Figure out the age of each person.

  In 10 years, Zak's age will be 136 less than four times the age of Jilly.

  The sum of the ages of Joe and David is 113.

  In 14 years, Jas's age will be 76 less than four times the age of Billie.

  Jas's age is 13 less than three times the age of Billie.

  Zak's age is 63 less than three times the age of Jilly.

  Joe is 37 years younger than David.

  David is 63 years older than Nishen.

  Solution: Zak is 66 years old, Nishen is 12 years old, Joe is 38 years old, Jilly is 43 years old, Billie is 21 years old, David is 75 years old, Jas is 50 years old.

Breakfast time

Breakfast time is an excellent activity for helping children understand how to work more logically by following a series of clues.

Suitable for

KS1
KS2

Aims

- Describe ways of solving puzzles and problems, explaining choices and decisions orally or using pictures.
- Explain reasoning using diagrams, graphs and text.
- To plan and pursue an enquiry.
- Explore patterns, properties and relationships.

Players

- This is an activity suitable for small maths groups

Resources

- Pencil and paper

What to do

- Introduce the problem as follows:

  Jade, Reshma, Hoshi and Keely each ate something different for breakfast. One had yogurt, one had cereal, one had sausages, and one had an egg for breakfast.

- Use the following clues in order to work out who had what for breakfast.

  Hoshi did not have yogurt or an egg for breakfast.

  Only Kaitlyn and Reshma like meat for breakfast.
  Jade did not have an egg for breakfast.

Jade likes to eat either cereal or yogurt for breakfast.
Keely did not have yogurt or cereal for breakfast.
Reshma likes to eat either an egg or cereal for breakfast.
Hoshi did not have an egg for breakfast.

- Using the clues given help children to draw up a simple table and then fill in what they know as they read the clues. Help them to complete the definite crosses first and build the rest of the table around that. For example, Keely had sausages for breakfast, Hoshi had cereal, Jade had yoghurt and Reshma had an egg for breakfast.

	yogurt	cereal	sausages	egg
Jade	✓	X	X	X
Reshma	X	X	X	✓
Hoshi	X	✓	X	X
Keely	X	X	✓	X

- Now set a similar problem and encourage children to complete a table in the same way as a scaffold for their clue-cracking. For example,

Meera, Holly, Rohit and Seth each ate something different for breakfast. One had sausages, one had cereal, one had yogurt, and one had toast for breakfast.

What did each person have for breakfast?

Meera likes to eat either yogurt or cereal for breakfast.
Rohit did not have yogurt or cereal for breakfast.
Holly did not have sausages for breakfast.
Holly did not have yogurt for breakfast.
Only Holly and Seth like meat for breakfast.

	sausages	cereal	yogurt	egg
Jade	X	X	✓	X
Reshma	X	✓	X	X
Hoshi	X	X	X	✓
Keely	✓	X	X	X

- Discuss how easy/difficult the problem was. Did using a table help to organise the information more readily?
- Discuss which clue groups started with, which clue came second, etc.

Variation

- This problem could be extended for any number of people. Here is a problem involving five people.

  Tam, Logan, Joaquin, Alvin and Afi each ate something different for breakfast. One had egg, one had croissants, one had cereal, one had yogurt, and one had bacon for breakfast.

  What did each person have for breakfast?

  Logan likes to eat either yogurt or bacon for breakfast.
  Only Alvin and Logan like meat for breakfast.
  Logan did not have croissants or egg for breakfast.
  Alvin did not have egg for breakfast.
  Alvin likes to eat either bacon or yogurt for breakfast.
  Alvin did not have yogurt for breakfast.
  Afi did not have yogurt or egg for breakfast.
  Alvin did not have pancakes for breakfast.
  Joquin did not have yogurt for breakfast.
  Tam did not have yogurt for breakfast.
  Joquin likes to eat either yogurt or cereal for breakfast.
  Solution: Alvin had bacon for breakfast, Joquin had cereal for breakfast, Afi had croissants, Tam had egg, Logan had yogurt.

Challenge questions

- Can you invent a breakfast problem using the names of your friends?
- Can you include redundant information in your clues to throw readers off the scent?

On your bike

On your bike is a great activity for helping children to think logically and how to join pieces of information together to form a whole.

Suitable for

KS1
KS2

Aims

- Describe ways of solving puzzles and problems, explaining choices and decisions orally or using pictures.
- Explain reasoning using diagrams, graphs and text.
- To plan and pursue an enquiry.
- Explore patterns, properties and relationships.

Players

- This is an activity suitable for small maths groups

Resources

- Pencil and paper

What to do

- Introduce the problem as follows:

  Andre, Oliver, Jozef and Miles each own a bicycle. One has a green bike, one has a blue bike, one has a white bike and one has a silver bike.

  Work out the colour of each person's bike.

  Oliver doesn't like white.
  Andre borrowed the green bike, because Oliver was using his bike.

Jozef doesn't like blue.

Miles doesn't like green.

Jozef doesn't like green either.

Miles borrowed the silver bike because Jozef was using his bike.

Andre's favourite colours are silver and blue. His bike is one of his favourite colours.

Jozef borrowed the blue bike, because Andre was using his bike.

Miles's favourite colours are green and white. His bike is one of his favourite colours.

- You could cut the clues up onto separate pieces of paper and tackle this as a whole class.
- Give each group a couple of clues each and go round each group asking for the information they have.
- As each group reads out the clues it has, a table can be completed so that children get to see how it is filled in step by step.
- Share the solution with children and recap.

	green	blue	white	silver
Miles	X	X	✓	X
Andre	X	✓	X	X
Oliver	✓	X	X	X
Jozef	X	X	X	✓

Miles has a white bike, Andre has a blue bike, Oliver has a green bike, and Jozef has a silver bike.

Variations

- This problem can be adapted for any object, e.g. pencils, bags, hats, etc.
- More children can be added to the problem as appropriate.
- You could set the challenge as a competition.
- Make a display of the problem and solution.
- Record children's problem-solving steps using a video camera and project onto the whiteboard.

Challenge questions

- Can you find a way of editing the number of clues so that there aren't so many but all of the information is retained?
- Can you act out the problem to make it easier for other groups to understand?

Shop, shop, shop!

Shop, shop, shop! is an activity for helping children to think calculate fractional amounts of money using logical reasoning.

Suitable for

KS1
KS2

Aims

- Describe ways of solving puzzles and problems, explaining choices and decisions orally or using pictures.
- Explain reasoning using diagrams, graphs and text.
- To plan and pursue an enquiry.
- Explore patterns, properties and relationships.

Players

- This is an activity suitable for small maths groups

Resources

- Pencil and paper

What to do

- Introduce the problem as follows:

  Abi, Josh, Cary and Dexter each went to the shopping centre with the money they had saved. They each had a different amount of money. Each person only spent a fraction of the money they started out with. They started out with: £8, £24, £64 and £32. At the shopping centre one spent $\frac{1}{4}$ of their money, one spent $\frac{1}{2}$ of their money, one spent $\frac{1}{8}$ of their money and one spent $\frac{3}{4}$ of their money.

- Set two problems for the children to solve:

  How much money did each person spend?

  How much money does each person have left?

- Read the following clues out for children to work with:

  Cary has £56 left after spending money at the shops.
  The person that started out with £8, has £2 left after shopping.
  Josh did not spend $\frac{3}{4}$ of his money.
  Dexter spent £16.

- Children can work in pairs to try and solve the problem using a table to help them structure their ideas.

- After a period of working take any feedback from children and discuss any issues arising from the problem.

- Work through the fractional amounts with children as appropriate and share the solution step by step as follows:

  Solution: Josh had £24 before going shopping. He spent $\frac{1}{4}$ of the money at the shops because he didn't spend $\frac{3}{4}$ of his money.

  Josh has £18 left.

  Dexter had £32 before going shopping because only one amount when halved would make 16 and that is 32. So, if Dexter spent $\frac{1}{2}$ of the money at the shops he still has £16.

  Abi had £8 before going shopping. We know she had £2 left which means she spent $\frac{3}{4}$ of her money since £2 = $\frac{1}{4}$.

  Cary had £64 before going shopping. Cary spent $\frac{1}{8}$ of the money at the shops.

  Cary still has £56.

Variations

- This problem can be adapted for other fractional amounts.
- Alter the amount of money spent in each case.
- Add more children to the problem to complicate it further.

Challenge question

- Can you find the solutions to this six-person problem?

  Luka, Shane, Zoe, Brett, Davina and Jonitha each had a different amount of money. They all went to the shopping centre and brought their money. At the shops, each person spent a fraction of the money they started out with. They started out with: £24, £88, £80, £40, £64 and £48.

  One spent $\frac{1}{2}$ of their money, one spent $\frac{3}{8}$ of their money, one spent $\frac{3}{4}$ of their money, one spent $\frac{7}{8}$ of their money, one spent $\frac{5}{8}$ of their money, and one spent $\frac{1}{8}$ of their money.

  How much money did each person spend?
  How much money does each person have left?

  Jonitha spent £36.
  Jonitha spent more than $\frac{3}{8}$ of her money.
  Shane has £55 left after spending money at the shops.
  The person that started out with £40, has £5 left after shopping.
  The person that started out with £64, has £24 left after shopping.
  Zoe has £21 left after spending money at the shops.
  Davina did not spend $\frac{1}{2}$ of her money.
  Zoe did not spend $\frac{7}{8}$ of her money.

Football stickers

Football stickers is an activity which encourages children to think between the lines and use a variety of clues to find the solution to a problem based on logic.

Suitable for

KS1
KS2

Aims

- Describe ways of solving puzzles and problems, explaining choices and decisions orally or using pictures.
- Explain reasoning using diagrams, graphs and text.
- To plan and pursue an enquiry.
- Explore patterns, properties and relationships.

Players

- This is an activity suitable for small maths groups

Resources

- Pencil and paper

What to do

- Introduce the problem as follows:

  Trey, Tommy, Nooria and Eve each started a football sticker collection. Each one of them collected a different number of stickers in May and June. During May, they collected 18, 33, 24 and 21 stickers and during June, they collected 47, 52, 42 and 46 stickers.

  Try to work out how many football stickers each person collected in May and June using the following clues:

If Trey did not collect stickers in May then Tommy would only have 47 stickers.

Nooria was not the one who collected 21 stickers in May.

Trey collected 24 more stickers in June than in May.

Eve has a total of 85 stickers.

- Groups can work with a different clue and the whole class can be responsible for solving the problem.
- Decide which clue to start with. Discuss why the second clue about Trey might be a good place to start.
- What clue would be a next best step? For example, what about the last clue? Which two numbers from May and June add together to make 85?
- Complete the solution together and agree as follows: Trey collected 18 in May and 42 in June, Tommy collected 21 in May and 47 in June, Nooria collected 24 in May and 46 in June, and Eve collected 33 in May and 52 in June.
- Discuss which was the hardest clue to unravel.
- Talk about the strategies that would be most helpful when solving this challenge.

Variations

- Adapt this problem to include 5, 6, 7, 8 or 9 children.
- Change the number of stickers collected by each.
- Choose something else for the children to collect, e.g. yogurt pots.

Challenge questions

- Is the month relevant to helping solve the problem? Can you include superfluous information within the clues already provided?

Pens

Pens challenges children to work out the number of pens a group of friends have using logical thinking and adopting a systematic way of working.

Suitable for

KS1
KS2

Aims

- Describe ways of solving puzzles and problems, explaining choices and decisions orally or using pictures.
- Explain reasoning using diagrams, graphs and text.
- To plan and pursue an enquiry.
- Explore patterns, properties and relationships.

Players

- This is an activity suitable for small maths groups

Resources

- Pencil and paper

What to do

- Introduce the problem as follows:
  Bina, Wing, Suki and Michelle each have a certain number of pens. One has 17 pens, one has 7 pens, one has 9 pens, and one has 5 pens.
  Try to work out how many pens each person has using the following clues:
  If Suki gave Bina 7 pens, Bina would have 14 pens and Suki would have 2 pens.
  Michelle is not the one with 17 pens.
  Wing and Michelle have 22 pens altogether.

- Decide whether to help children structure the problem or let them find their own strategy.
- If using a table, get the children to tell you what the headings should be and how it should be completed. For example, putting a cross in Michelle and 17 is an obvious starting point. If Wing and Michelle have 22 pens altogether then we are looking for 2 numbers adding together to make 22; 17 + 5.

	17	7	9	5
Bina				
Wing	✓	X	X	X
Suki				
Michelle	X	X	X	✓

- Share the solution with children and either complete a table or write the answers on the board as follows:

  Solution: Wing has 17 pens, Bina has 7 pens, Suki has 9 pens, and Michelle has 5 pens.

- Which clue was the hardest to start with? Was there enough information to complete the table with just three clues?
- How does one clue lead to another?

Variations

- Substitute any other object for pens.
- Change the names of the pupils to your own class names.
- Change over the column and row headings so the table can be read in more than one way.

Challenge question

- Can you include three more clues to the problem above that would help to solve the problem? For example, you might say, 'Bina has a prime number of pens.' Try to be creative without being too challenging.

Pizza the action

Pizza the action challenges children to use their problem-solving prowess to work out pizza toppings eaten by a group of friends. It tests their ability to decipher information, work with clues and read between the mathematical lines.

Suitable for

KS1
KS2

Aims

- Describe ways of solving puzzles and problems, explaining choices and decisions orally or using pictures.
- Explain reasoning using diagrams, graphs and text.
- To plan and pursue an enquiry.
- Explore patterns, properties and relationships.

Players

- This is an activity suitable for small maths groups

Resources

- Pencil and paper

What to do

- Introduce the problem as follows:

  Catlin, Justine, Dinah and Fiona visit Pizza the action restaurant together. They each choose different pizzas. One chooses cheese, one has pepperoni, one has a veggie pizza, and the other has anchovies. Can you work out which person has which pizza based on the following clues?

Dinah likes meat.
Fiona is a vegetarian.
Justine has an allergy to milk products.
Catlin doesn't like seafood.

● Look carefully at the clues together and decide the best way of gathering and presenting the information.
● Decide that drawing a table is the most organised way of building a picture of who ate what.
● Draw the table on the board and ask for volunteers to label the rows and columns.
● Complete the table clue by clue using ticks and crosses inside the table as follows:
● Discuss the results and how to read the table. Are children confident reading it?

	cheese	**pepperoni**	**veggie**	**anchovies**
Catlin	✓	X	X	X
Justine	X	X	X	✓
Dinah	X	✓	X	X
Fiona	X	X	✓	X

Variations

● Replace the pizza names with ones of your own choosing.
● Include more children in the problem.
● Include three completed tables done by other groups which contain mistakes and challenge the children to find them.

Challenge questions

● Can you prepare a logical problem like this using 6 people and 6 pizzas?
● Can you ensure that you have included enough clues for the problem to be solved?
● Think about the strategy of creating a table to show the information in the table – is there another way to solve this problem?

Race to it

Race to it involves children thoroughly reading a series of clues and understanding each one in order to visualise a problem and its solution.

Suitable for

KS2

Aims

- Describe ways of solving puzzles and problems, explaining choices and decisions orally or using pictures.
- Explain reasoning using diagrams, graphs and text.
- To plan and pursue an enquiry.
- Explore patterns, properties and relationships.

Players

- This is an activity suitable for small maths groups

Resources

- Pencil and paper

What to do

- Introduce the problem as follows:

  Dallas, Annie, Blake, Connor and Elliott had a race across the playground. Can you work out who came first, second, third, fourth and fifth using the clues below?

  Annie didn't finish in last position.
  Connor wasn't in first or last place.
  Dallas finished just in front of Blake.
  Elliott didn't finish just before or after Connor.

Blake wasn't last.
Connor did not finish just before or just after Blake.
Dallas finished just in front of Blake.

- This may be a difficult problem for many children because of the wording so you may need to have mixed ability groups helping each other.
- You could give each group all the clues or you might decide to give each group a clue so that everyone helps each other.
- Discuss why drawing a grid would be a convenient way of visualising the information.
- Clarify the steps needed in order to solve the problem.
- Discuss whether certain clues offer more scope than others or whether they can be approached in any order.
- Draw up a table and ask groups to have a go at completing it themselves.
- Compare and contrast answers between groups and then show the solution – how close were children to solving it?

	1st	2nd	3rd	4th	5th
Dallas	X	X	✓	X	X
Annie	✓	X	X	X	X
Blake	X	X	X	✓	X
Connor	X	✓	X	X	X
Elliott	X	X	X	X	✓

Variations

- Use true and false or yes and no to clarify each step rather than ticks or crosses.
- Add bogus clues that are not important to solving the clue.
- Combine some of the clues so there are fewer to read.

Challenge questions

- Which clue did you start with?
- Can you place the clues in order according to how helpful they were when completing the table?
- Can you prepare a similar problem with more children in the race?

Chapter 7
Number tricks

What a card

What a card is a great number mind-reading trick which uses quite simple numbers to produce impressive results.

Suitable for

KS2

Aims

- To recognise numbers and their properties.
- To investigate how a number trick works.

Players

- Suitable for pairs, small groups or the whole class

Resources

- Pencil and paper

What to do

- Write the following rows of numbers on the board:

  Line A   1 3 5 7 9 11 13 15 17 19 21 23 25 27 29 31
  Line B   2 3 6 7 10 11 14 15 18 19 22 23 26 27 30 31
  Line C   4 5 6 7 12 13 14 15 20 21 22 23 28 29 30 31
  Line D   8 9 10 11 12 13 14 15 24 25 26 27 28 29 30 31
  Line E   16 17 18 19 20 21 22 23 24 25 26 27 28 29 30 31

- Ask children to look at the numbers carefully. Now ask someone to select a number that appears on one of the lines but they shouldn't tell you what it is.
- Ask the pupil selecting the number to say which lines the number appears on.

- When you are told the lines that the number appears on you will be able to 'read their mind' and say what the number was. For example, let's say that the number 5 was chosen. The pupil would say 'My number appears on lines A and C. Without hesitation you are able to say, 'I think your number is 5.'
- Have a few more demonstrations of your number powers and then ask children to work out how they think you might do the trick.
- Reveal to children that the trick is to always look at the starting numbers on each line to work out the number thought of. So, if the pupil chose 5 and said it was on lines A and C then you would need to look at the beginning of line A (1) and the beginning of row C (4) and add these two numbers together.

Variations

- Let children perform the trick with a friend before trying it with a group.
- Use the number lines to find the range.
- Use the number line for number recognition purposes. For example, what number am I? I am a number in line A. Both my digits are prime and my digital root is 6.

Challenge questions

- How can the trick go wrong?
- Will the trick always work?
- What connection can you find between the number lines? Do they all add up to make the same sum? Why do they all end in 31?
- Why doesn't the trick work if you look at the end of the number lines and add? Why must you always look at the beginning of the lines and add to reveal the number thought of?
- Can you add a new line to the trick? What numbers would you include? Does it work?

Too good to be true!

Too good to be true! is an impressive number trick which helps children record their answers and use a calculator.

Suitable for

KS2

Aims

- To practise following complex instructions.
- To use a calculator with more understanding.

Players

- Suitable for pairs, small groups or the whole class

Resources

- Pencil and paper
- Calculator

What to do

- Tell children that you have written a number inside an envelope (2000) which will be revealed at the end of your number trick. Say that the number will be a number that everyone will have.
- Give out the calculators and ask children to get ready to follow a series of instructions.
- Ask children to select a 4-digit number. For example, 1234.
- Now add 2999 (4233)
- subtract 39 (4194)
- add 3.1 (4197.1)
- subtract 7.9 (4189.2)
- subtract 899 (3290.2)
- add 1.8 (3292)

- subtract 58 (3234)
- subtract your original number (2000)
- Now reveal what is inside your envelope and ask children to say what number they have.
- Now write the steps of the trick on the board or photocopy and ask children to try this number trick again with some other 4-digit numbers.

Variation

- A nifty variation of this trick is to follow these steps:

  Select a 4-digit number (5874)
  Add 4999 (10873)
  Add 5.1 (10878.1)
  Subtract 99 (10779.1)
  Subtract 9.9 (10769.2)
  Subtract 699 (10070.2)
  Add 2.8 (10073)
  Subtract 199 (9874)
  Subtract the number you started with (4000)

Challenge questions

- Can you perform your own number trick like this and perform it to another group?
- Do all 4-digit numbers work for this trick? What about numbers that are all the same?
- Can you store your answer using the M+ button?

Eleven's heaven

Eleven's heaven is a wonderful trick for multiplying by 11.

Suitable for

KS2

Aim

- To practise multiplying 2-digit numbers by 2-digit numbers.

Players

- Suitable for pairs, small groups or the whole class

Resources

- Pencil and paper

What to do

- Tell children that multiplying by 11 is the easiest 2-digit number to multiply by because your answer will always begin start and end with the same numbers as the one you're multiplying by 11. For example, 11 x 14 = 154.
- Demonstrate how the trick works using the following example,

  Separate the two digits in your mind (1__4).
  Notice the hole between them!
  Add the 1 and the 4 together (1+4 = 5)
  Put the resulting 5 in the hole 154. That's it! 11 x 14=154

- Demonstrate with another example: 11 x 25 = 275. How? Separate the 3 and 5 making sure to leave a space between them. Now add 2 and 5 to make 7. Place the 7 in the gap and you get 275.
- Let children try a couple by themselves, e.g. 11 x 32, 11 x 45.

- Now show children what happens when in the next example. Write 11 x 58 on the board and ask them to try the trick they have just learned using this method. Does it work? Explain why 5138 cannot be the correct answer. Now show what to do:

  If the result of the addition is greater than 9, you only put the 'ones' digit in the gap and carry the 'tens' digit from the addition. For example 11 x 58 ... 5_8 ... 5+8 = 13. Put the 3 in the gap and add the 1 from the 13 to the 6 in to get 6 for a result of 638.

- Now practise some examples where the addition is greater than 9.

Variations

- Hold a speed test with children where they have to multiply various numbers by 11 in the fastest time possible.
- Hold a demonstration session whereby children from different groups showcase the trick to each other.
- Invite children to write their method for x 11 for a maths poster.

Challenge questions

- Does this trick work for any other number apart from x 11? Try the trick for other numbers such as x 12, x 22, etc.
- Does this trick work for 3-digit numbers? For example, 11 x 321. Would this achieve a correct answer?

Number scan

> Number scan is a clever, multi-step trick that involves children adding, multiplying and subtracting.

Suitable for

KS2

Aims

- To practise using addition, subtraction and multiplication skills.
- To follow a set of instructions.
- To investigate how a number trick works.

Players

- Suitable for pairs, small groups or the whole class

Resources

- Pencil and paper

What to do

- Demonstrate the trick to children.
- Ask children to write down two numbers, one less than 10 and one more than 10, e.g. 7 and 38.
- Now add them together (45).
- Multiply by 5 (225).
- Add the smaller number (232).
- Multiply by 2 (464).
- Subtract the smaller number again (457).
- Now subtract 1 (456).

- Tell children that you will be able to tell what their original numbers were. In order to do this you add 1 to the result (457) – the units digit represents the smallest number. To work out the number more than ten subtract 7 from 45 to get 38.
- Talk through the example and do the same for two other numbers to see how the trick works.
- Children then try the trick for themselves using their own numbers.

Variations

- Let children perform this trick in front of the class once they become confident.
- Another variation of this trick works as follows:
  1. Write down two numbers one less than 10 and one more than 10, e.g. 7 and 16.
  2. Multiply the second number by 10 (160).
  3. Multiply the first number by 9 (63).
  4. Subtract the two numbers (97).
  5. You can now reveal the two numbers – the units digit is 7 and the larger than 10 number is 9 + 7 = 16).

Challenge questions

- Why does one number always have to be under 10?
- Will this trick work for any number over 10? What about numbers over 99?

Catch-22

Catch-22 is a very clever number trick that involves combining 2-digit numbers, adding and dividing skills.

Suitable for

KS2

Aims

- To practise using addition and division skills.
- To follow a set of instructions.
- To investigate how a number trick works.

Players

- Suitable for pairs, small groups or the whole class

Resources

- Pencil and paper
- Calculators

What to do

- Tell children that you have a number written inside an envelope that you think will match a number that someone in the class will have after they have followed some simple instructions.
- Tell everyone to follow these steps:
  Write down any three numbers less than 10. For example, 2, 5 and 8.
  Now make all the six possible 2-digit numbers using these numbers: 25, 28, 52, 58, 82, 85.
  Now add them together (330).
  Find the sum of the original three numbers (2 + 5 + 8 = 15).
  Divide the first sum by the second (330 ÷ 15).
- Get everyone to keep their number as secret as possible.
- Now ask everyone to write down their number on their whiteboard.
- Open up the envelope to reveal the number 22.

Variation

- Try this trick to make the number 23 by following these steps:
  write down any 3 digits e.g. 373
  add 25 (398)
  multiply by 2 (796)
  subtract 4 (792)
  divide by 2 (396)
  subtract your original number (23)

Challenge question

- Could you make this trick work for six possible 3-digit numbers? For example, if you chose 3, 6 and 7 then you could make 367, 376, 763, 736, 637 and 673. Adding these together would make 3552. If you add 3, 6 and 7 you get 16. Then 3552 divided by 16 makes 222.

High five

High five is a neat number trick that involves doubling, adding, subtracting and halving skills.

Suitable for

KS1
KS2

Aims

- To practise using addition, subtraction, doubling and halving.
- To follow a set of instructions.
- To investigate how a number trick works.

Players

- Suitable for pairs, small groups or the whole class

Resources

- Pencil and paper

What to do

- Tell children that you have a number written inside an envelope that you think will match a number that someone in the class will have after they have followed some simple instructions.
- Tell everyone to follow these steps:
  1. Write down any number between 1 and 10.
  2. Double it.
  3. Add 10.
  4. Double it.
  5. Subtract 10.
  6. Halve it.
  7. Subtract your original number.

- Get everyone to keep their number as secret as possible.
- Now ask everyone to write down their number on their whiteboard.
- Open up the envelope to reveal the number 5.

Variations

- Perform the trick with just one person at a time until the class start to see that the same answer is reached each time!

Challenge questions

- Will this trick work for numbers between 1 and 15?
- Why is doubling important to the trick?
- By adding 10 and subtracting 10, what are you effectively doing?
- Could you make this trick work for a number other than 5? For example, to make 6 each time, follow these steps: write down any number, double it, add 20, subtract 8, divide by 2, subtract your original number.

Your number is...

> Your number is... is one of many number mind-reading tricks that combines simple multiplication and addition.

Suitable for

KS1
KS2

Aims

- To practise using addition and multiplication.
- To follow a set of instructions.
- To investigate how a number trick works.

Players

- Suitable for pairs, small groups or the whole class

Resources

- Pencil and paper

What to do

- Tell children that you are a great mind-reader of numbers and you will attempt to guess anyone's number.
- Tell children to follow these steps:

  Write down any number between 1 and 9.
  Multiply by 2.
  Add 1.
  Multiply by 5.

- When children have got that far, ask anyone to say what number they have. Let's say that someone started with 6 and followed the steps above then they would end up with 65. When they tell you 65, tell them confidently that their number is 6.

- Repeat this a few times for other children to participate in.
- Challenge everyone to work out how the trick is done and whether they have spotted a pattern.
- Reveal the method behind the trick: in order to work out the number originally thought of, look at the tens digit that the player says at the end of the steps above. Always look at the tens and that will reveal the number.

Variations

- Reveal the number by writing it down rather than saying it, e.g. put it inside an envelope.
- Get groups to perform the trick for others and judge who is the most effective.

Challenge questions

- Can you see how the trick works? Try retracing the steps backwards.
- Will this trick work for decimal numbers such as 1.5?
- Will this trick work for numbers between 1 and 20?
- Will the trick work if you multiply by other numbers?

Two little ducks

> Two little ducks is a very clever number trick that combines addition and division of 2-digit numbers.

Suitable for

KS2

Aims

- To practise using addition and division.
- To follow a set of instructions.
- To investigate how a number trick works.

Players

- Suitable for pairs, small groups or the whole class

Resources

- Pencil and paper
- Calculators

What to do

- Ask children to write down any 3-digit number in which the digits are all different, for example 123.
- Get them to show you on their whiteboards.
- Now ask children to write down all the possible 2-digit combinations of the three digits used and add them together. So 123 would make $12 + 13 + 23 + 21 + 31 + 32 = 132$.
- Point out to children that when adding the digits there should always be six possibilities – can they work out why?
- Now add the digits in the original number chosen. For example, $1 + 2 + 3 = 6$.

- Now divide the sum of the two-digit numbers (132) by the sum of the digits in the original number (6). So $132 \div 6 = 22$
- The answer will always be 22.
- Repeat this for other 3-digit numbers.

Variations

- Roll a 1-6 dice or a 4-9 dice three times to make a 3-digit number.
- Try this trick with a 3-digit number in which two of the digits appear twice, e.g. 454. How many combinations of 2-digit numbers are possible? Does this end in 22?

Challenge questions

- Will this trick work for any 3-digit number? What happens if the digits are all the same?
- What happens if one of the three digits is a zero?
- Can you make this trick work for a four-digit number?

Seven steps

Seven steps is an amazing number trick that combines all four operations and is ideal for improving mental maths skills.

Suitable for

KS2

Aims

- To practise using the four operations and numbers with any number of digits.
- To follow a set of instructions.
- To investigate how a number trick works.

Players

- Suitable for pairs, small groups or the whole class

Resources

- Pencil and paper
- Calculators

What to do

- Ask children to choose any number less than 100, e.g. 45. Tell them that you are going to turn their number into the number 7 by following various calculations that they have to follow and perform as you say them.
- First subtract 2 from your number (45 – 2 = 43)
- Multiply by 3 (43 x 3 = 129)
- Add 12 (129 + 12 = 141)
- Divide by 3 (141 ÷ 3 = 47)
- Add 5 (47 + 5 = 52)
- Subtract the original number (52 – 45 = 7)
- Try this trick again for other numbers.

Variations

- Try doing this trick work for 3-digit numbers.
- Repeat the trick for numbers with four digits.
- What connection is there between the number 7 and the operational steps? How does the trick work?

Challenge questions

- Will this trick work for any number with any number of digits?
- Will this trick work using decimal numbers?
- Will this trick work for negative numbers?

3-digit wonder

> 3-digit wonder is a great division trick that will have everyone scratching their heads.

Suitable for

KS2

Aims

- To practise division of a large number.
- To read and write whole numbers.
- To practise using a calculator.

Players

- Suitable for pairs, small groups or the whole class

Resources

- Calculators

What to do

- Ask children to think of any 3-digit number, e.g. 472.
- Ask them to repeat the number in order to make a 6-digit number, e.g. 472, 472. Say and write the number.
- Now get children to type the 6-digit number into their calculator and divide by 13. Children record their answer.
- Now divide by 11 and record your answer.
- Finally divide by 7.
- The number you now have should be the 3-digit number you started with. If it isn't then go through each step again.
- Discuss with children how the trick works.
- Repeat the trick for other numbers.

Variations

- Try doing this trick work for all 3-digit numbers.
- Get children to teach and perform this trick to others.

Challenge questions

- Is there a connection between 13, 11 and 7 that makes this number trick work?
- If you add 13, 11 and 7 to get 31, does dividing a 6-digit number by 31 give the same answer?
- Can you make this trick work for 4-digit numbers?

Magic 6174

Magic 6174 is a neat number trick that combines subtraction and the reordering of digits.

Suitable for

KS2

Aims

- To practise subtraction.
- To investigate how a number trick works.

Players

- Suitable for pairs, small groups or the whole class

Resources

- Pencil and paper
- Calculators

What to do

- Ask children to choose any four numbers from 0 to 9.
- Now ask them to arrange those digits to make the largest 4-digit number they can.
- Tell children that you are going to turn their number into 6174.
- Ask children to follow your instructions as follows:
  1. Write your 4-digit number.
  2. Now rearrange the digits to make the smallest possible number.
  3. Subtract the smallest number from the largest.
  4. Now arrange the digits of this answer to make the largest possible answer.

5. Arrange the digits to make the smallest possible answer.
6. Subtract the smallest from the largest.
7. Keep repeating these steps until you end up with the number 6174.

Variations

- Try this trick for a 4-digit number where all the digits are the same, e.g. 5555.
- Ask one of the children to demonstrate this trick to the rest of the class.

Challenge questions

- Does this number trick work for all 4-digit numbers? Are there any numbers it won't work for, e.g. consecutive numbers such as 1234? Will it work for numbers that contain two zeros such as 2,020? Will the number trick work for any numbers made up of certain numbers? For example, does a number containing all square numbers work such as 1,149?
- If you followed the same repeating pattern of steps as above with a 3-digit number taking the smallest from the largest, what number would you end up with?
- Which numbers can be turned into 6174 in the fewest steps? Can you spot a pattern?

Magic pentagons

Magic pentagons is just for fun but includes an element of investigation.

Suitable for

KS1
KS2

Aims

- To practise simple addition.
- To investigate how a number trick works.

Players

- Suitable for pairs, small groups or the whole class

Resources

- Four numbered pentagons (see below)

What to do

- Show the class the four numbered pentagons (these need to be drawn so that pentagon 1 has the following numbers in each corner – 1, 6, 7, 8, 10 and a number one printed in the centre, pentagon 2 = 9, 6, 5, 10, 7 and a 2 printed in the middle, pentagon 3 = 5, 6, 8, 9, 10 and a three printed in the middle, pentagon 4 = 4, 10, 7, 9, 8 and a 4 printed in the centre).
- Ask for a volunteer.
- Ask the volunteer to select a number found on one of the vertices of any pentagon and to point to all of the pentagons this appears on.
- Now reveal that you will be able to predict what the number selected is.

- Ask children to work out how you are able to seemingly read the mind of the volunteer.
- Reveal how you were able to say the number – by adding the middle numbers of the pentagons pointed to you are able to unearth the volunteer's selected number.

Variation

- Use different numbers to make your own Magic pentagon puzzle.

Challenge questions

- Is there a connection between the centre number and numbers on each corner?
- Is there a connection between each pentagon?
- Can this trick work for more than four pentagons?
- Will this trick work for other shapes such as hexagons? heptagons? octagons? and so on?

Mind reader!

Mind reader! is a great activity for playing with numbers and helping children to practise some maths magic.

Suitable for

KS1
KS2

Aims

- To practise simple addition and subtraction.
- To foster number confidence and mental agility.

Players

- An activity for two players

Resources

- 5 dice (1–6 dice)

What to do

- Tell the class that you can see through solid objects!
- Throw five dice and say that you can read the bottom numbers without having to lift the dice off the table.
- Say the five bottom numbers and announce their total when added together. For example, if you threw a 2, 5, 3, 1 and 2 announce confidently that the bottom numbers are 5, 2, 4, 6 and 5 and that the total of these numbers is 22.
- Explain to the class your secret! Say that on any 1–6 die, the sum of the top number and the bottom number is always 7. So, if five dice are thrown then the total of all the top and bottom numbers is 35.

- Now get children to have a go themselves.
- One player in the pair throws five dice and then says what the numbers are underneath each die. This player's partner can turn them over and check.
- Players take it in turns throwing the dice, saying what numbers are underneath and adding them together. The total of the bottom numbers is the number of points scored for that round.
- The winner is the player who has the most points after six rounds of playing.

Variations

- This game activity can be played with an increasing number of dice.
- For the five numbers thrown create some new rules. For example, if you throw two sixes in one throw then you miss a go.

Challenge questions

- Would this game work for dice that have more than six sides? Investigate different dice and find out.
- What do the numbers on a 1–6 die add up to? Why do the top and bottom numbers add up to 7?

Maths master

Maths master is an impressive multiplication trick that is challenging, entertaining and mind-boggling.

Suitable for

KS1
KS2

Aims

- To practise mental arithmetic skills.
- To foster number confidence and mental agility.
- Describe and explain methods, choices and solutions to puzzles and problems.

Players

- Independent, pairs, small groups and the whole class

Resources

- Pencil and paper
- Calculators
- Number cards 0–9
- Die

What to do

- Demonstrate this number trick to the class first.
- Ask someone to give you a 3-digit number. For example, 428.
- Write this number down twice as follows
  428   428
- Now ask for another 3-digit number. For example, 736. Write this number underneath one of the 428s.
  428   428
  736

- Calculate in your head the number which, when added to 736, gives 999, which in this example is 263. Pretend you are thinking of another number at this point and write 263 under the other 428.

428	428
736	263

- Tell children that you are going to multiply 428 by 736 and then add that to the product of 428 and 263. Say you will do this in your head!
- Provide the answer of 427,572 within seconds.
- Share with children the 'secret' to this trick as follows:

  The first 3 digits of the answer are $428 - 1 = 427$.
  The next three digits are the digits added to 427 to make 999, i.e. 572.

- Now get children to try this trick for themselves with a partner.

Variations

- Randomly select a number by using number cards or a die.
- Ask a table group to work through an example ready to show the rest of the class.

Challenge questions

- Does this trick still work for numbers like 111, 222, 333, etc.?
- Does this trick work for consecutive numbers such as 123, 234, 345, etc.?
- Does this trick work for consecutive odd numbers such as 1, 3, 5?
- Why does the 3-digit number have to be added to give 999?
- Does this number trick work with 2-digit numbers and adding to 99?
- Does this number trick work for 4-digit numbers and adding to 9999?

Name your number

Name your number is a very impressive 'mind-reading' trick that is fun and thought-provoking involving some simple addition skills.

Suitable for

KS1
KS2

Aims

- To practise mental arithmetic skills.
- To foster number confidence and mental agility.
- Describe and explain methods, choices and solutions to puzzles and problems.

Players

- Independent, pairs, small groups and the whole class

Resources

- Whiteboard and pen
- Pencil and paper
- Name your number, number boards

What to do

- Give children each a copy of the number boards below and ask them to study the boards carefully for patterns.

Board 1

3	5	7	9	11	1
13	15	17	19	21	23
25	27	29	31	33	35
37	39	41	43	45	47
49	51	53	55	57	59

Board 2

5	6	7	13	12	4
14	15	20	21	22	23
28	29	30	31	36	37
38	39	44	45	46	47
52	53	54	55	60	13

Board 3

9	10	11	12	13	8
14	15	24	25	26	27
28	29	30	31	40	41
42	43	44	45	46	47
56	57	58	59	60	13

Board 4

3	6	7	10	11	2
14	15	18	19	22	23
26	27	30	31	34	35
38	39	42	43	46	47
50	51	54	55	58	59

Board 5

17	18	19	20	21	16
22	23	24	25	26	27
28	29	30	31	48	49
50	51	52	53	54	55
56	57	58	59	60	31

Board 6

33	34	35	36	37	32
38	39	40	41	42	43
44	45	46	47	48	49
50	51	52	53	54	55
56	57	58	59	60	46

- Ask for a volunteer to select a number on one of the boards, any number. The number must not be revealed.
- Ask the person selecting the number to see if the number they have chosen also appears on any of the other number boards.
- Ask your volunteer to point to the number boards that their number appears on. Again, the chosen number cannot be revealed. For example, they may point to boards 1, 3 and 4.
- Tell the class that you will read the mind of the volunteer and write down on a whiteboard the number that person has selected. If they have selected boards 1, 3 and 4, you can confidently reveal that their number is 11.
- Repeat this trick a few times to wow your audience and then reveal the trick.
- The trick works like this: for each of the boards pointed to, all you have to do is add the numbers that appear in the top right corner.

Variations

- You could use individual boards as target boards for practising a variety of skills. For example, using Board 1 you could say, how many prime numbers are there in the second column? What is the difference in totals between row 1 and row 5? etc.
- Ask children to learn the trick themselves and perform to the rest of the class.

Challenge questions

- How does this trick work? Is there any connection between the top right corner numbers? What do they add up to?
- What do the individual boards add up to?
- Can you invent your own number board trick like this where the top left numbers are added together to reveal the chosen number?

Number head

Number head is an amazing 'mind-reading' trick that will impress any audience. This stunning trick involves some basic maths and can be learnt with practice by a range of learners.

Suitable for

KS1
KS2

Aims

- To practise mental arithmetic skills.
- To foster number confidence and mental agility.
- Describe and explain methods, choices and solutions to puzzles and problems.

Players

- Independent, pairs, small groups and the whole class

Resources

- Pencil and paper
- Number head number grid

What to do

- Give children a copy of the Number head grid shown on page 242.
- Tell everyone that you have memorised every single number on the board and that you'd like to challenge someone.
- Ask for a volunteer to select a number in bold and say that you will write down the number that appears underneath it. For example, if they select 5, confidently write down 6178538.
- Repeat this a few times to prove that luck isn't involved.

- Build tension into your performance by slowing down the way you recite and write numbers.
- Challenge the class to work out how the number trick works. Take feedback from groups and see what they suggest.
- Reveal the method behind the trick as follows

1. Add 11 to the number selected
2. Reverse the result
3. Keep on adding the two previous numbers leaving out the 10s
4. Say the number.

For example, if 1 was selected, add 11 to get 12. Reverse 12 to get 21. Now add 2 and 1 to get 3, 1 and 3 to get 4, 3 and 4 to get 7, 4 and 7 to get 11 (but ignore the 10 – just write down 1), add 7 and 1 to get 8.

If 5 is chosen, then add 11 to make 16. Now reverse the digits to make 61. Then add 6 and 1 to get 7. 7 and 1 to get 8. 8 and 7 to get 15 but ignore the ten part of 15. Now add 8 and 5 to get 13 and ignore the 10. Finally add 5 and 3 to get 8. The number is 6178538.

23	39	18	22	4	38	16
4370774	0550550	9213471	3369549	5167303	9437077	7291011
2	**45**	**30**	**34**	**25**	**6**	**15**
3145943	6516730	1459437	5493257	6392134	7189763	6280886
9	**37**	**46**	**3**	**1**	**17**	**32**
0224606	8426842	7527965	4156178	2134718	8202246	3471897
21	**5**	**44**	**11**	**41**	**19**	**8**
2358314	6178538	5505505	2246066	2572910	0336954	9101123
29	**12**	**33**	**13**	**43**	**7**	**10**
0448202	3257291	4482022	4268426	4594370	8190998	1235831
49	**14**	**24**	**47**	**26**	**40**	**28**
0662808	5279651	5381909	8538190	7303369	1561785	9325729
31	**27**	**35**	**48**	**20**	**42**	**36**
2460662	8314594	6404482	9549325	1347189	3583145	7415617

Variations

- Instead of using the whole number board, which may be too much for some learners to look at, cut out just the first row of numbers and focus on these.
- Use the number board to practise other skills, e.g. look at the number that appears under 30, now say that number. Reverse the digits and say the number you have made. Add the digits and multiply it by 30. How many numbers underneath 30 are factors of 30? How many square numbers can you see underneath 30? Which number in the row of numbers under 30 is the odd one out?

Challenge questions

- Can you invent a row of numbers to join the number board? Think of a number and then follow the method above to make the number underneath.
- What is the name given to the number sequence whereby neighbouring numbers are added to each other in this way?

Chapter 8
Mixed problems

Bingo·bingo

Bingo-bingo is an interactive bingo game designed to help children improve their general mental arithmetic skills.

Suitable for

KS1
KS2

Aims

- Add or subtract mentally combinations of numbers.
- Use practical and informal written methods to multiply and divide numbers.
- Use knowledge of place value and multiplication facts to 10 x 10, the corresponding division facts and multiples of numbers to 10 up to the tenth multiple.

Players

- A game for the whole class

Resources

- Bingo cards
- Bingo-bingo 0–100 resource question sheet

What to do

- Give children a copy of the Bingo cards or ask them to draw a grid, five columns by four rows as shown here.

0-20	21-40	41-60	61-80	81-100

- Tell children then to write down 15 numbers. Column 1 can contain numbers between 1 and 20, column 2 numbers between 21 and 40 and so on.
- Select one of the bingo cards and read out the problem for children to solve. For example, 5 squared – 12. If children have the answer 13 written in the correct column on their bingo card, they cross that number off or cover with a counter.
- Encourage children to volunteer their answers so that you can pick up any misunderstandings.
- The winner is the player who crosses all their numbers off and calls out 'Bingo-bingo!'

Variations

- The questions can be tailored according to the groups you are teaching to make them more or less demanding.
- You could add a fourth row to your bingo card.
- Children could play with more than one card.
- Children make up the next question if they answer correctly.
- Number ranges could be changed, e.g. 1–15, 16–30 and so on.

Challenge questions

- Can you invent your own questions for the Bingo-bingo game?
- Can you include bonus numbers? For example, if you score 25 then you can cross off any other number between 21 and 40.

Bingo-bingo 0-100 resource sheet

0	1	2	3	4	5
10 x 0	23 minus 22	4 – 2	2 + 1	2 lots of 2	35 ÷ 7
3 squared minus 9	11 + 11	The first even prime	$\frac{1}{3}$ of 9	24 ÷ 6	$\frac{1}{4}$ of 20
24 – 2 dozen	100 – 99	Square root of 4	The first odd prime	The second square number	The third prime number
	1 squared	100 ÷ 50	10 less than a baker's dozen	The square root of 16	10% of 50

6	7	8	9	10	11
4 squared – 10	56 ÷ 8	The square root of 64	3 squared	1000 ÷ 100	The fifth prime number
2 squared + 2	Square root of 49	48 ÷ 6	The square root of 81	The square root of 100	A fifth of 55
Square root of 36	The fourth prime number	2 lots of 4	The third square number	2.5 x 4	29 – 18
54 ÷ 9	93 – 86	2 cubed	108 ÷ 12	a dozen – 2	9.5 + 1.5

12	13	14	15	16	17
A gross + 12	7 + 6	7 x 2	15% of 100	Half of 32	17 % of 100
A baker's dozen minus 1	The second 2-digit prime	84 ÷ 6	7.5 x 2	The fourth square number	51 + 3
$\frac{1}{4}$ of 48	26 ÷ 2	50% of 28	60 ÷ 4	4 squared	9 add 8
8 x 1.5	A score minus 7	65 – 51	105 – 90	96 ÷ 6	8 less than 25

18	19	20	21	22	23
Double 9	38 divided by 2	A score	50 – 29	50% of 44	A score plus 3
3 lots of 6	4 squared plus 3	4 lots of 5	7 lots of 3	5 squared minus 3	2 dozen minus 1
2 less than a score	One less than a score	3 squared plus 11	$\frac{1}{3}$ of 63	2 lots of 11	50% of 46
6 more than a dozen	21 minus the first even prime	400 ÷ 20	105 ÷ 5	132 ÷ 6	30 minus the 4th prime

24
A baker's dozen plus 11
120 ÷ 5
The mode of 23, 22, 24, 24, 22, 24
6 lots of 4

25
¼ of 100
5 squared
200 ÷ 8
17 + 8

26
A baker's dozen x 2
13 x 2
⅓ of 78
100 – 74

27
9 x 3
3 x 3 x 3
83 – 56
100 – 73

28
The product of 4 and 7
34 – 6
2 lots of 14
The number of days in 4 weeks

29
116 ÷ 4
36 – 7
2 dozen plus 4
Double 14.5

30
6 x 5
⅓ of 90
Number of days in September
270 ÷ 9

31
Number of days in May
15.5 divided by 2
A score + 10
100 – 69

32
2 x 2 x 2 x 2 x 2
8 lots of 4
50 – 18
32 – 14

33
11 times the second prime
50% of 66
18 more than a dozen
100 – 67

34
17 x 2
102 ÷ 3
34% of 100
40 – 6

35
5 x 7
50% of 70
⅓ of 105
210 ÷ 6

36
6 x 6
6 squared
9 lots of 4
50% of 72

37
¼ of 148
40 minus the second prime
6 squared plus 1
100 – 63

38
19 x 2
50 – 12
9.5 x 4
114 + 3

39
13 x 3
50 – 11
7 squared minus 10
30 + 9

40
2 score
8 lots of 5
50% of 80
240 + 6

41
Double 20.5
A score plus 3 x 7
37 + 4
13 x 3 then add 2

42
2 lots of 21
6 lots of 7
50 minus 8
⅓ of 126

43
100 – 57
30 plus a baker's dozen
The second prime number more than 40
55 –12

44
11 lots of 4
88 divided by 2
14 more than 30
176 ÷ 4

45
9 x 5
45% of 100
100 – 55
2 score plus 5

46
92 divided by 2
26 plus a score
138 ÷ 3
6 squared plus 10

47
100 – 53
Next prime after 43
2 score plus 7
8 more than 39

48
12 lots of 4
1000 – 952
6 x 8
9 lots of 5 plus 3

49
7 squared
50 minus the first square number
50 minus the first cube number
50 minus the first triangular number

50
50% of 100
200 ÷ 4
2 score and 10
⅕ of 250

51
Treble 17
30 more than 21
47 plus the second square number
100 – 49

52
26 x 2
The number of weeks in a year
25 x 2 then add 2
520 + 10

53
The next prime number after 47
50% of 100 add three
60 minus 7
17 + 36

54
9 lots of 6
27 x 2
1000 – 946
50 plus the second square number

55
55% of 100
5 lots of 55
3 score less 5
165 ÷ 3

56
7 lots of 8
28 x 2
7 squared + 7
8 squared minus 8

57
60 minus 3
50 plus the 4th prime
8 more than 49
19 x 3

58
29 x 2
55 + second prime
100 – 42
232 ÷ 4

59
Second square number plus 11 x 5
3 score minus 1
7 squared plus 10
9 more than 50

60
6 lots of 10
3 lots of 20
4 lots of 15
8 lots of 7.5

61
4 plus 57
1000 – 939
Number of days in January and April
30.5 doubled

62
31 x 2
40 add 22
Number of days in January and July
100 – 38

63
21 trebled
9 lots of 7
3 more than 3 score
144 – 81

64
8 squared
9 squared – 17
10 squared – 6 squared
12 squared – 80

65
7 x 5 plus 30
13 x 5
32.5 x 2
100 – 35

66
6 lots of 66
3 lots of 22
198 ÷ 3
150 – 84

67
70 minus the 1st odd prime
40 plus 27
Next prime after 61
3 score + 7

68
34 x 2
9 squared minus a baker's dozen
8 more than 60
272 ÷ 4

69
23 x 3
70 minus 1 squared
90 less than the first 2-digit prime
138 ÷ 2

70
7 lots of 70
9 squared minus 11
35 x 2
2 score plus 30

71
100 – 29
1000 – 929
10000 – 9929
35.5 x 2

72
12 lots of 6
6 squared plus 6 squared
6 dozen
18 x 4

73
$\frac{1}{5}$ of 365
100 – 27
The next prime after 71
Double 36.5

74
80 minus 6
37 x 2
70 plus the second square number
34 + 2 score

75
75% of 100
$\frac{3}{4}$ of 100
8 squared + 11
70 + 3rd prime

76
80 minus 4
38 x 2
100 – 2 dozen
12 x 6 then add 4

77
11 lots of 7
38.5 doubled
85 minus the second prime
76 plus the first cube number

78
26 x 3
80 minus the first prime
125 – 47
150 – 72

79
75 plus 2 + 2
4 x 4 x 4 then add 15
Double 39.5

80
4 score
8 lots of 10
$\frac{4}{5}$ of 100
80% of 100

81
40.5 x 2
9 squared
100 – 19
3 x 3 x 3 x 3

82
150 – 68
9 squared plus 1
Double 41
79 add the second prime number

83
50 add 33
41.5 x 2
9 squared plus the first prime
The next prime after 79

84
100 – 16
4 more than 4 score
90 minus 6
7 lots of 12

85
17 x 5
100 – 15
42.5 x 2
$\frac{1}{3}$ of 255

86
1000 – 914
120 – 34
43 x 2
10 less than 100 – 4

87
29 x 3
50 plus 37
90 – the 2nd prime number
174 divided by 2

88
2 lots of 44
90 minus the first prime
10 squared minus 1 dozen
A gross – 56

89
100 – 11
1000 – 911
44.5 x 2
11 squared – 32

90
9 lots of 10
10 squared minus 10
9 squared + 9
89 + 1 squared

91
9 squared + 10
100 – 3 squared
120 – 29
45.5 x 2

92
23 x 4
46 x 2
92 x 1 squared
100 – 8

93
89 plus 2nd square number
50 + 43
150 – 93
56 + 37

94
55 + 39
9 squared + 15
47 x 2
10 squared minus 6

95
45 plus 50
17 x 5
47.5 x 2
120 – 25

96
48 x 2
24 x 4
12 x 8
6 x 16

97
The largest 2 digit prime
44 + 53
100 minus the 2nd prime
48.5 x 2

98
50 + 48
100 minus the 1st prime
120 – 22
196 divided by 2

99
3 lots of 33
297 + 3
11 lots of 9
10 squared minus
1 squared

100
10 squared x 1
One gross minus 44
5 score
12 x 8 plus the second square number

Bango-bango

Bango-bango is a bingo-style game intended to support children develop their mental arithmetic skills.

Suitable for

KS2

Aims

- Add or subtract mentally combinations of numbers.
- Use practical and informal written methods to multiply and divide numbers.
- Use knowledge of place value and multiplication facts to 10 x 10, the corresponding division facts and multiples of numbers to 10 up to the tenth multiple.

Players

- A game for the whole class

Resources

- Bingo-style cards
- 0–9 number cards

What to do

- Give children a copy of the Bingo cards or ask them to draw a grid, five columns by five rows as shown here.

- Children then write the numbers 1–25 anywhere on the grid, for example:

5	16	9	21	2
18	4	19	17	8
11	12	1	7	23
14	24	15	20	25
3	22	6	13	10

- Now select three cards from a well-shuffled pack of 0–9 digit cards.
- Challenge children to make the numbers on their grid using the three digit cards drawn. When a number has been made then that number is crossed off.
- The winner is the first player who can make any row of numbers.

Variations

- Increase the size of the grid from 5 x 5 to 6 x 6, 7 x 7, 8 x 8, etc.
- The winner could be the first person to cross off the numbers in a column, a diagonal, or get a full house.

Challenge questions

- Can you invent a similar game in which the numbers in the grid are all prime numbers?
- Can you work out whether it makes a difference or not if the numbers in the grid are placed randomly?

Colour by numbers

Colour by numbers is an exciting game that combines all four operations in a colourful number square.

Suitable for

KS1
KS2

Aims

- Use knowledge of number properties to solve problems.
- Identify and use patterns, relationships and properties of numbers.

Players

- An activity for 3 players

Resources

- Four 1–6 dice
- A 1–100 number grid
- Coloured counters

What to do

- Ask children to get into threes and give them a copy of the coloured 1–100 number grid shown on page 255:
- Players each receive six coloured counters.
- Players take it in turns to throw four dice.
- The dice are combined to make a number on the 1–100 grid using any operation. For example, if you threw a 5, 5, 2 and 6 then you could simply add them to make 18 or you could multiply the 5 and 5, multiply the 2 and 6, add the two totals together and cover 37. You could divide 5 and 5, divide 6 by 2 and then subtract these totals to make 2. There are lots of combinations.

- In order to play more strategically, the boxes are all tinted and score points as follows: black = 12 points, white = 8 points, grey = 6 points and light cyan = 3 points.
- Play continues until everyone has placed all of their counters.
- The player with the most points is the winner.

1	2	3	4	5	6	7	8	9	10
11	12	13	14	15	16	17	18	19	20
21	22	23	24	25	26	27	28	29	30
31	32	33	34	35	36	37	38	39	40
41	42	43	44	45	46	47	48	49	50
51	52	53	54	55	56	57	58	59	60
61	62	63	64	65	66	67	68	69	70
71	72	73	74	75	76	77	78	79	80
81	82	83	84	85	86	87	88	89	90
91	92	93	94	95	96	97	98	99	100

Variations

- Play this game with fewer numbers. For example, play with numbers 1–50.
- Play with three dice instead of four.
- Play with five dice but only four are chosen.
- Play with three 1–6 dice and three operations dice.
- Change the colour code score or introduce new colours with a higher value. Perhaps have one pink square that is worth 25 points for example.
- You can play this game according to whether a number is square or prime. For example, any prime number covered scores 2 points whereas a square number squares 4 points.
- Any number where the tens digit is double the units digit scores double.
- You can place a counter on a number already covered by one of your counters but not someone else's.

Challenge questions

- Can you write down all of the factors of the numbers you have covered?
- How many of your numbers have a digital root of 1?
- Can you play the game where the object is to cover numbers with 4 factors?

Row by row

> Row by row tests children's knowledge and understanding of number properties.

Suitable for

KS1
KS2

Aims

- Use knowledge of number properties to solve problems.
- Identify and use patterns, relationships and properties of numbers.

Players

- An activity for small groups

Resources

- Whiteboards and pens
- A number table

What to do

- Ask children to look at the number table shown here.

Row 1	1	2	3	4	5
Row 2	6	7	8	9	10
Row 3	11	12	13	14	15
Row 4	16	17	18	19	20
Row 5	21	22	23	24	25
Row 6	26	27	28	29	30
Row 7	31	32	33	34	35

- What do they notice about the numbers? Can they find any patterns in the way numbers are arranged?
- Now challenge children to write down two numbers from the table that are a) prime numbers, b) square numbers, c) multiples of 7, d) factors of 36.
- Discuss answers together. Now ask children to find the total of the numbers in row 1 and the total of the numbers in row 2. What is the difference between them? Repeat this for rows 2 and 3. Is the difference between the two totals the same as before?
- Ask children to explain why the difference between the total of row 3 and 4 will be 25 again.
- Now challenge children to work out whether the difference between consecutive rows will be 25.

Variations

- You can ask a variety of questions relating to number properties such as, 'How many prime numbers are there in row 4?', True or False, there are 2 triangular numbers in the first three rows,' etc.
- Add more numbers to each row and see what difference that makes to the above investigation.

Challenge questions

- Add up the numbers in consecutive columns – what is the difference between them? Is there a pattern?
- If you add up blocks of four numbers what totals do you get? Can you find a connection between blocks of four numbers?
- Can you spot patterns in each row and column?

Weigh to go

Weigh to go is a great activity for investigating how much you weigh in relation to the masses of some British coins.

Suitable for

KS1
KS2

Aims

- Use knowledge of number properties to solve problems.
- Identify and use patterns, relationships and properties of numbers.
- Make decisions, cooperate and test ideas.

Players

- An activity for small groups

Resources

- Whiteboards and pens
- 1p, 2p, 5p, 10p, 20p, 50p, £1, £2 coins
- Bathroom scales
- Calculators

What to do

- Show children some British coins. Give each group some coins so they can touch and feel.
- Ask children to write the values of the coins from 1p to £2 on a piece of paper in a table as shown on page 259 or provide a photocopied sheet.
- Now ask children to estimate the mass of each coin.

Coin	Estimated mass (g)	Actual mass (g)	Difference (g)
1p			
2p			
5p			
10p			
20p			
50p			
£1			
£2			

- When children have discussed their ideas, see what answers children decided upon and share the actual masses of the coins.
- Now challenge children to work out the differences between their estimates and the actual masses.
- Now ask for one of the children to volunteer. Say that you will need to weigh the volunteer.
- Ask the volunteer to step onto some bathroom scales and then record the weight on the board. For example, 36kg.
- Ask children to think about how many grams 36kg is.
- Challenge the class to work out how much this person is worth in £2 coins.
- Talk about ideas for finding out the information. Discuss plans and then give children time to do their calculations. Calculators are allowed.
- When children have worked out an answer compare and contrast ideas and see whether there is agreement or disagreement.
- In the example above, someone weighing 36kg would be worth £3,000 because 36kg = 36,000g and 36,000g ÷ 12g = 3,000.

Coin	Estimated mass (g)	Actual mass (g)	Difference (g)
1p		3.56	
2p		7.13	
5p		3.25	
10p		6.5	
20p		5	
50p		8	
£1		9.5	
£2		12	

Variations

- Children can work out how much they are worth.
- Work out how much you are worth for the other British coins.
- Try working out how much you are worth in another currency.
- Weigh the coins to double-check the accuracy of the masses given.

Challenge questions

- Can you find the width and thickness of each coin in millimetres?
- Can you draw up a table of results to show how much you are worth from 1p to £2?
- How much are you worth if you add your weight in 1p to £2?
- What are the accurate mathematical names for the front and back of a coin? (the side showing the Queen's head is called the obverse and the other side is the reverse).

See this

> See this is a brilliant activity for improving children's mathematical visualisation skills.

Suitable for

KS1
KS2

Aims

- Use knowledge of number properties to solve problems.
- Identify and use patterns, relationships and properties of numbers.
- Make decisions, cooperate and test ideas.

Players

- An activity for small groups

Resources

- Whiteboards and pens
- Pencil and paper

What to do

- Tell children that you want them to close their eyes and listen to your instructions.
- Start by asking children to imagine a 1–6 die. Ask them to see the die on a table in front of them. Keep your eyes closed.
- Now imagine that the number five is the number on the top of the die. What number is touching the table?
- Remind children that the opposite faces of a 1–6 die always add up to 7 so that the number touching the table should be a number 2.
- Now ask them to imagine the number 1 facing them as they look down. What number is opposite this? (6)

- Ask children to now imagine throwing two dice and they land on the table as a double 4. What numbers are touching the table (double 3s)?
- Mentally throw the dice again. This time the numbers are 5 and 4. Find the total of these dice (9) and then multiply by the total of the numbers touching the table (2 + 3 = 5, 9 x 5 = 45).
- Clear your mind. Now throw three dice. The numbers thrown are 2, 4, 6. Add these together and add to the total of the numbers touching the table (2+ 4 + 6 = 12; 5 + 3 + 1 = 9; 12 + 9 = 21).
- Now imagine throwing a die on its own. The number you throw is a 6. What do the numbers round the sides add up to? (6 is on top and 1 is on the bottom, leaving 2, 3, 4, 5 making 14 when added together).
- Now ask children to open their eyes and talk about their experience of doing this activity. Did they find it easy? Difficult? Was it getting easier to do?

Variations

- Judge how well children cope with the activity then introduce a fourth die and ask similar questions in order to test children's visualisation skills. Perhaps start with one die.
- Ask questions relating to addition, subtraction, multiplication and division.
- You could try this activity for different types of dice.

Challenge questions

- Can you throw five dice mentally and add up the totals round the sides if the numbers thrown are 2, 3, 4, 5, 5?
- Can you invent your own dice visualisations? Can you think of combining dice with another mathematical object? For example, dice and a 1–100 number grid. What questions could you think of combining these two? Try to think of ten questions for another group to try.

Digital delight

Digital delight is a group activity for encouraging children to work collaboratively on a problem using the digital clock.

Suitable for

KS1
KS2

Aims

- Read and use 24-hour clock notation.
- Make decisions, cooperate and test ideas.

Players

- An activity for small groups

Resources

- Whiteboards and pens
- Pencil and paper
- Digital clocks

What to do

- Show children a digital clock and ask them what they notice about the numbers. Can they see that the individual digits are made up of bars?
- Ask children how many bars they can see? (28)
- Write a digital clock time on the board using bars. For example, 09:13 and ask them to count the bars (19).
- Ask children to tell you the following information in relation to 09:13:

  How many vertical lines can you see? (11)
  How many horizontal lines can you see? (8)
  How many right angles can you see? (16)
  What is the product of the digits? (0 x 9 x 1 x 3 = 0)

- Now write another digital time on the board and ask the same questions, e.g. 17:23.
- Point out that 17:23 was made up of 15 bars. Set children the challenge of finding as many other times with 15 bars. How many can they find? For example, 17:46, 15:10, 19:15, etc.

Variations

- Investigate digital times and the number of bars, right angles, etc. for a variety of other times.
- If each bar on a clock measured 6mm, what would be the total measurement for the time 18:39? Try asking this for various other times.

Challenge questions

- Can you turn the 24-hour clock times you have made into 12-hour clock times?
- How many digital clock times are there with 19 bars?
- Which time uses the most bars?
- Which time uses the least bars?

On your marks

On your marks is a problem-solving activity involving number patterns.

Suitable for

KS1
KS2

Aims

- Describe number patterns in words.
- Devise and use problem-solving strategies to explore situations mathematically.

Players

- An activity for small groups

Resources

- Whiteboards and pens
- Pencil and paper

What to do

- Tell children the following mathematical story: Two grasshoppers, Splat and Splot, decided to have a race at the 100m track. Splot starts at 1m and Splat starts at 30m. Splot can jump three numbers at a time and Splat can jump two. If they both jump together, who will get to the 100m line first and how long do they have to wait for the other one?
- Now ask children to work together in groups of three to discuss their ideas about how to solve the problem.
- Ask children to think about the numbers in Splat's pattern and the numbers involved in Splot's pattern.

- Discuss different ways of solving the problem and talk about the efficiency of each one. For example, compare acting it out with drawing up a table.
- Draw up a table of results to show that Splot would get to the 100m line first and have to wait two jumps for Splat to catch up.

	0	1	2	3	4	5	6	7	8	9	10
Splat	30	32	34	36	38	40	42	44	46	48	50
Splot	1	4	7	10	13	16	19	22	25	28	31

	11	12	13	14	15	16	17	18	19	20	21
Splat	52	54	56	58	60	62	64	66	68	70	72
Splot	34	37	40	43	46	49	52	55	58	61	64

	22	23	24	25	26	27	28	29	30	31	32
Splat	74	76	78	80	82	84	86	88	90	92	94
Splot	67	70	73	76	79	82	85	88	91	94	97

	33	34	35
Splat	96	98	100
Splot	100		

Variations

- This problem could be acted out if you have the space available in the school grounds.
- Alter the jump sequence and see what difference other jump sizes make.

Challenge questions

- If Splat starts at 51m and jumps two numbers at a time and Splot starts at 1m and jumps 4m every time, who would be first to 100?
- If Splat starts at 27m and jumps 3m every time and Splot starts at 7m and jumps 4m every time, who would be first and how long would the other grasshopper have to wait?

Take it away

Take it away is a problem-solving activity involving number patterns.

Suitable for

KS1
KS2

Aims

- Select and use a problem-solving strategy.
- Identify patterns used in solving the problem.
- Devise and use problem-solving strategies.

Players

- An activity for two players

Resources

- Whiteboards and pens
- Pencil and paper
- Coloured counters

What to do

- Each pair of players has five counters and then places them in a row.
- Players then take turns, removing one or two counters each turn.
- The person to remove the last counter is the winner.
- Challenge children to find a game strategy so that the first player always wins.
- What do they notice when playing the game?
- If you are the first player how many counters should you take and why? Ask children whether they think this is a fair game or not. Remind them that in a fair game, each player has an equal chance of winning.
- Share strategies for playing the game.

Variations

- Play the game 'Take three or less' and place 21 counters in a row. In pairs, take turns to remove one, two or three counters each turn. The person to remove the last counter is the winner.
- Change the number of counters that can be taken to one, two, three or four.

Challenge questions

- What happens if you change the number of counters to 33?
- Can you find a way of winning involving any number of counters or is a game like this just luck?

Maths adder

Maths adder helps children to practise the addition of 2-digit numbers and encourages them to share the methods that they use to solve the problem.

Suitable for

KS1
KS2

Aims

- To add a range of 2-digit numbers.
- Make decisions, cooperate and test ideas.

Players

- An activity for small groups

Resources

- Whiteboards and pens
- Pencil and paper
- Calculators

What to do

- Ask children to write down any 2-digit number.
- Now ask children to reverse the digits to make another 2-digit number.
- Add the two numbers together.
- Discuss with the students the strategies that they could use to add 2-digit numbers.
- Let children work on the problem individually before organising into small groups.
- How many answers do you get which are still 2-digit numbers?

- Children team up with a partner to work together. Ask children how they could organise their reversed numbers so that they could look for patterns in the answers.
- What do the answers have in common?
- Share solutions together. There are many patterns that can be found. For example,

13 + 31 = 44
16 + 61 = 77
98 + 89 = 187
56 + 65 = 121

- If the sum of the digits in the 2-digit number is less than 10 then the sum of the reversed numbers is less than 100.

17 + 71 = 88

- Can children invent a statement to say what they notice? For example, the sum of the digits in a 2-digit number determines the sum of the reversed numbers: if the sum is 8 the answer is 88, if the sum is 4 then the sum of the reversed numbers is 44.

Variation

- Investigate as many numbers as possible and record any patterns as statements.

Challenge questions

- What counting methods did you use/could you use to add the numbers together?
- Is there a pattern in the numbers that give 3-digit sums?
- What statements can you write for other sums?

Take five

Take five helps children to practise the addition of 1- and 2-digit numbers and encourage them to share the methods that they use to solve the problem.

Suitable for

KS1
KS2

Aims

* Recognise number properties, e.g. odd, even, prime, square, composite, cube, etc.
* Devise and use problem-solving strategies (use equipment).
* Make decisions, cooperate and test ideas.

Players

* An activity for pairs

Resources

* Whiteboards and pens
* Pencil and paper
* Calculators

What to do

* Ask children to think of any five numbers between 1 and 99 inclusive and then write them in ascending order. Remind them what ascending and descending mean.
* Now ask children to add the first number to the second; the second and the third; the third and the fourth; and the fourth and the fifth.

- Score points as follows: every odd number made is worth three points; every even number is worth five points; every square number is worth 7 points.
- What is the highest score that you can get? In how many ways can you get it?
- What is the lowest score that you can get? In how many ways can you get it?
- Share findings and solutions with each other.

Variations

- Change the number of numbers that you use.
- Change the number of points.
- Change the range of numbers that you use.
- Use other number properties like cube numbers, numbers divisible by 6, and so on.
- Change the operation from addition to multiplication, subtraction or division.

Challenge questions

- What counting methods did you use/could you use to add the numbers together?
- The highest number of points that you can get is 12. Is it possible to get every number from 0 to 12 as the result of choosing some five-number set?
- How do you know that the number is a square number?
- Can you convince me that this number is a cube number?

How many?

How many? will help children to spot patterns and relationships within the context of a number problem.

Suitable for

KS2

Aims

- Devise and use problem-solving strategies.
- Make decisions, cooperate and test ideas.

Players

- An activity for pairs

Resources

- Whiteboards and pens
- Pencil and paper

What to do

- Pose the problem for children to solve: how many 2-digit numbers are there that contain at least one 2?
- Let children work in pairs to share ideas and discuss plans to solve the problem.
- Check solutions and approaches used.
- Discuss why listing the numbers systematically is the most efficient way of solving the problem. There are eighteen 2-digit numbers: 12, 20, 21, 22, 23, 24, 25, 26, 27, 28, 29, 32, 42, 52, 62, 72, 82, 92.
- Now ask children to think about how many 3-digit numbers there are that contain at least one 3.
- Ask children questions that focus on the rules of divisibility.
- Share solutions and encourage children to think about the approaches used by other pairs. Which do they think are more efficient than the approach they used?

Variations

- Investigate how many 5-digit numbers there are that contain at least one 5.
- Let children work in bigger groups for more demanding investigations so they can share the workload and responsibility.

Challenge questions

- Is it easier to count all 3-digit numbers that don't contain a 3?
- Can you write a formula for finding the answers to the above investigations?
- When writing the numbers from 1 to 150, how many times do you write the digits 2, 6 and 7? (2 = 35, 6 = 25, 7 = 25)

Circle sums

Circle sums is a great problem for performing a variety of calculations in an interesting and challenging context.

Suitable for

KS1
KS2

Aims

- Recall basic addition facts to 20.
- Investigate odd and even numbers.
- Devise and use problem-solving strategies.
- Make decisions, cooperate and test ideas.

Players

- An activity for pairs

Resources

- Whiteboards and pens
- Pencil and paper

What to do

- Get children to draw 9 circles in a 3 x 3 array.
- Now introduce the problem to everyone: write the numbers 1–9 inside the circles so that the sums of the three numbers on each side are a) all different sums b) all the same sums c) all even sums d) all odd sums.
- Read the problem again and make sure that everyone understands that they can use each of the numbers 1–9 once only.
- Discuss ideas and continue until the circles are full.
- Share answers to each of the parts of the problems.
- Ask children to make statements about the combination of odd and even numbers.

Variations

- Investigate how many 5-digit numbers there are that contain at least one 5.
- Let children work in bigger groups for more demanding investigations so they can share the workload and responsibility.

Challenge questions

- Can you arrange the numbers so that all the rows and columns have the same sum? How many ways can you do this?

Fair enough

Fair enough is an interesting game that helps children to get to grips with the concept of fairness and probability.

Suitable for

KS1
KS2

Aims

- Understand and use the probability scale from 0–1.
- Find and justify probabilities based on equally likely outcomes in simple contexts.

Players

- An activity for pairs

Resources

- Whiteboards and pens
- Pencil and paper
- Counters
- 2 dice
- Probability track

What to do

- Give pairs of children the following track.

Win				Start				Lose

- Players take it in turns to throw two dice and work out the difference between their scores.
- If the difference is 0, 1 or 2, then move one square to the left and place your counter on the appropriate square.

- If the difference is 3, 4 or 5 then move one square to the right.
- Play the game until someone reaches the Win or Lose square.
- Play the game a few times.
- Is the game fair? Discuss opinions and try to reach agreement.

Variations

- The number of squares on either side of the start square could be changed. You could include another two squares on either side.
- Throw one die and the number of spaces moved is equal to the number opposite the number thrown. For example, if a 5 was thrown then 2 spaces would be moved.
- Play odds and evens. For example, if the difference is odd then move to the right. If the difference is even then move to the left.

Challenge questions

- Can you work out the probability of moving one space to the left? One space to the right?
- Would the game be fair if there were 6 squares to the left of Start and only 4 squares to the right?
- Can you invent a game using a horizontal track combined with a vertical track?

A good match

A good match is a thought-provoking activity that encourages children to problem-solve using matchsticks.

Suitable for

KS1
KS2

Aims

- Devise and use problem-solving strategies.
- Make decisions, cooperate and test ideas.

Players

- An activity for individuals or pairs

Resources

- Whiteboards and pens
- Pencil and paper
- Headless matchsticks

What to do

- Give children some headless matchsticks and ask them to make the shape on page 280.
- Now challenge children to move just two of the matchsticks to form 7 squares.
- Remind children that you said 'move' rather than 'remove' and that other matchsticks cannot be added to the shape.
- Children may make a shape with 7 squares but the shape has to be complete, i.e. there shouldn't be any matchsticks sticking out from the shape.

- After a while, share solutions or attempts. Has anyone solved the problem?
- Show children how to solve the problem as shown here.

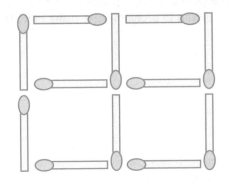

Variations

- Using the same window shape made up of 12 matchsticks, set children the challenge of moving 4 matchsticks to make 10 squares.
- Using the window design again, move 2 matchsticks to make 3 squares and 6 rectangles.
- Using the window design, move 4 matchsticks to make 3 squares.

Challenge questions

- Can you invent your own matchstick problem with matchsticks?
- How many right angles can you see? How many parallel lines? How many perpendicular lines? How many diagonal lines? How many oblique lines? How many congruent shapes?

Chapter 9
Investigations

Always, sometimes, never true

Always, sometimes, never true encourages children to explore a mathematical statement and find specific evidence to prove its validity.

Suitable for

KS1
KS2

Aims

- Explore patterns, properties and relationships and propose a general statement involving numbers or shapes.
- Identify examples for which the statement is true or false.

Players

- An activity for small group discussion

Resources

- Whiteboards and pens

What to do

- Write the following statement on the board and ask children to think about it individually: 'Multiplication makes a number bigger.'
- Now ask children in their groups to share their ideas about the statement to see if they agree or disagree.
- After a period of discussion tell children that it is their job to prove or disprove the statement with specific examples to other groups.
- After more discussion, children elect someone from their group who acts as the group envoy. This person swaps places with the envoy from another group and the envoys then share in the discussions of other groups.

- The envoys return to their own groups after 5 minutes and share the thinking they have just listened to.
- Come together as a whole class and ask groups to volunteer their thoughts and the statement is debated. For example, 'We think multiplying by one means the number stays the same', 'We think that the number will get smaller if you multiply by a fraction', and so on.
- After discussing one statement, investigate another such as 'Dividing will always make a smaller number.'

Variations

- There are various statements to investigate. You could present children with a collection of 'Number' statements, 'Shape' statements and so on, or choose to theme them. For example, you might select to focus on decimal and fraction statements such as 'A decimal number with three digits is bigger than one with two digits', '$\frac{2}{6}$ is equal to 0.3', 'There are 6 tenths in $\frac{3}{5}$', '$\frac{1}{4}$ is more than 0.251', '$\frac{9}{12}$ is greater than $\frac{3}{4}$', and so on.
- Present children with 3–6 statements to discuss rather than one.
- Make a display of the statements discussed and place children's responses around them.

Challenge questions

- Can you invent your own statements for another group to discuss?
- How many times do you have to prove something in order to say whether you think a statement is true or false?

Number theft

> Number theft is an excellent activity for helping children to think logically and strategically.

Suitable for

KS1
KS2

Aims

- Use knowledge of the four operations to solve problems.
- Refine and use efficient written methods to add, subtract, multiply and divide.

Players

- An activity for 2 players

Resources

- Whiteboards and pens

What to do

- Tell children that someone has stolen the numbers 1, 2, 4, 6, 7, and 8 leaving only 3, 5 and 9.
- Now challenge children to use 3, 5 and 9 to make all the numbers from 1–30 using any of the four operations. For example, 9–5 = 4, 4–3 = 1.
- Digits can be joined together. For example, 3 and 4 could make 34.
- The first pair to find all the numbers from 1–30 are the winners.

Variations

- You could try this investigation with any three numbers. For example, say that the numbers 1, 2 and 3 have been stolen.
- Instead of 1–30, challenge children to make up to 40.
- Instead of three numbers being stolen, have four numbers.

Challenge questions

- Is it possible to make numbers from 1 to 50 using only the three digits 3, 5, and 9?
- Is it possible to make the numbers from 1 to 40 using only three of the operations?
- Investigate whether it is possible to make the numbers from 1 to 40 just using combinations of three odd numbers and compare that to combinations of three even numbers.

Number stacks

Number stacks is an addition-based investigation activity that encourages children to search for patterns.

Suitable for

KS1
KS2

Aims

- To report solutions to puzzles and problems, giving explanations and reasoning orally and in writing.
- Collect, organise and interpret selected information to find answers.

Players

- An activity for individuals, pairs and small groups

Resources

- Number stacks resource sheet

What to do

- Share with children the Number stacks sheet as follows
- Talk about each number stack and what children notice about the numbers, both vertically and horizontally.
- Now suggest to children that you think that any number in Stack C added to Stack E will always make a number in Stack B. Do they agree? How many times would you need to test this in order to say it was true or false?

- Challenge children to look for other number stacks that may have a similar relationship. What do they notice? Can they make a number stack statement such as 'Any number in Stack A added to....'?
- Can children invent their own number stack problem but using number stacks where the difference is 6?

Stack A	Stack B	Stack C	Stack D	Stack E
0	1	2	3	4
5	6	7	8	9
10	11	12	13	14
15	16	17	18	19
20	21	22	23	24
25	26	27	28	29
30	31	32	33	34
35	36	37	38	39
40	41	42	43	44
45	46	47	48	49
50	51	52	53	54
55	56	57	58	59

Variations

- This activity lends itself well to investigating number stacks where the difference between numbers is 7, 8, 9 or more.
- Number stacks can be created for other number patterns, e.g. Fibonacci, square numbers, triangular numbers, cube numbers and so on. Number stacks don't have to have the same pattern – try one stack of one pattern, another stack of another pattern and so on.

Challenge questions

- Can you complete this table in relation to the Number stacks problem?

	A	B	C	D	E
A					
B					
C					b
D					
E					

Add up blocks of four numbers and see what new patterns you can make. For example, what do you notice about the numbers in each block here?

0	1
5	6

1	2
6	7

2	3
7	8

3	4
8	9

Slide and hop

Slide and hop is a fun activity that encourages children to think about patterns, working systematically and communicating with each other in a clear and logical way.

Suitable for

KS1
KS2

Aims

- To look for patterns, predict and test results.
- To look for reasons why rules work and to prove formula.

Players

- An activity for small groups and the whole-class.

Resources

- Coloured counters
- Grid tracks

What to do

- Show children the following grid track and two counters (labelled A and B here but red and blue counters can be used)

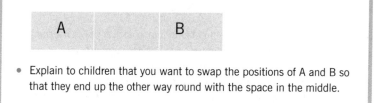

- Explain to children that you want to swap the positions of A and B so that they end up the other way round with the space in the middle.

- The rules are as follows:
    1. The counters can only move one at a time.
    2. There can only be one counter on a square at any one time.
    3. The counters can slide onto the adjacent square.
    4. The counters can only jump over one counter at a time.
- Show that this simple example would take only three moves for the counters to swap sides.
- Now ask children to work out what the smallest number of moves would be for two counters to swap sides. Give them an empty track and four counters, two of one colour and two of another.

- Now try three counters of each colour. Challenge children to complete the task in 15 moves and to record their moves on paper. Can they record the number of jumps, number of slides and total number of moves in a table?
- After children have worked on the problem for a while, share ideas and discuss the moves made.

Variations

- This activity is perfect for acting out using chairs. Try two boys and two girls to start with then progress on to three boys and girls.
- You set this investigation as a table challenge to see who can solve it first.
- Try 4 counters, 5 counters and so on. Challenge children to predict the minimum number of moves needed when six counters of each colour are used.

Challenge questions

- What do you notice about the number of jumps each time? Is it a prime number of jumps? A square number? A triangular number?
- Can you write a formula for solving this problem?
- Can you graph your results to the investigations above?
- What about investigating an unequal number of counters on each side? How does this make a difference?
- What about having two spare squares in the middle? How does this make a difference?

Get in shape

> Get in shape is an activity that will really get children thinking about two-dimensional shapes and their component angles.

Suitable for

KS1
KS2

Aims

- Use knowledge of properties to draw 2-D shapes.
- Draw shapes with increasing accuracy.

Players

- A whole-class activity completed independently

Resources

- Whiteboards and pens
- Square dotty paper
- 2-D shapes
- Rulers and pencils

What to do

- Ask children to draw a pentagon on their whiteboards. Don't state whether the pentagon is regular or irregular.
- Get children to show you what they have drawn by asking table groups one at a time to hold up their whiteboards.
- Discuss the shapes drawn. What are the similarities and differences between them? Did most people draw the same shape?

- Show children some 2-D shapes and focus particularly on the pentagon. Talk about whether it is regular or irregular and name the angles between vertices.
- Now challenge children to think about a pentagon differently. Ask them to draw a pentagon with one right angle. Use square dotty paper. What do children draw?
- Now challenge children further to find out whether a pentagon can have two, three or four right angles?
- When children have investigated the pentagon challenge, discuss the shapes drawn and try to reach an agreement about the shapes.

Variations

- This activity could be repeated for other shapes. For example, can children draw a hexagon with 3, 4 and 5 right angles?
- Ask children to think about drawing other 2-D shapes with right angles but focus on internal right angles and external right angles.

Challenge questions

- Is it possible to tessellate a regular pentagon?
- What are the total of the angles in a quadrilateral? pentagon? hexagon? heptagon? etc.
- What do you notice about shapes with an odd or even number of sides?
- Can you draw a table or sorting diagram to show the maximum number of right angles 2-D shapes can have? Use your results to spot a pattern.
- How many right angles can a decagon have?

Water butt

Water butt is a fantastic visualisation activity that demands children to think outside the box. This can be solved by drawing or acting out the problem.

Suitable for

KS2

Aims

- Plan and pursue and enquiry.
- Explain reasoning using diagrams, graphs and text; refine ways of recording using images and symbols.

Players

- A whole-class activity or small groups

Resources

- Whiteboards and pens

What to do

- Explain that you have an empty water butt and two buckets, one 5-litre bucket and an 8-litre bucket.
- Say to children that you want to fill the water butt up with exactly 18 litres of water and to do that you would need to fill the 5-litre bucket twice and the 8-litre bucket once.
- Now set the challenge of filling the water butt with exactly 7 litres. How would you do it? Split children into small groups and set them off on the challenge explaining that they can draw their answer or act it out.
- After 10 minutes discuss any solutions that may have been found. Talk about how difficult the task is and what problems the children found.

- Share the answer: fill the 5-litre bucket three times and pour the water into the water butt. Then drain off 8 litres from the water butt into the 8-litre bucket. This leaves 7 litres in the water butt because 15 litres – 8 litres = 7 litres.
- Now set children the challenge of getting 3 litres of water.

Variations

- Work out ways of obtaining quantities of water from 1 litre up to 25 litres.
- You could try this problem by altering the volume of the buckets. For example, suppose you have one bucket of 7 litres and another bucket that holds 9 litres. Get children to work out ways of obtaining quantities of water from 1 litre to 25 litres.

Challenge questions

- Can you invent your own water butt problem with different size buckets?
- What about a problem involving three buckets?

Shape up

Shape up is an activity that will prompt children to think about the area of rectilinear shapes.

Suitable for

KS2

Aims

- Draw and measure lines to the nearest millimetre.
- Measure and calculate the area of regular shapes.
- Calculators
- Use the formula for the area of a rectangle to calculate the rectangle's area.

Players

- A whole-class activity completed independently

Resources

- Whiteboards and pens
- Square dotty paper
- Rulers and pencils

What to do

- Show children a simple picture of a rectangle without any measurements.
- Ask children what the measurements could be.
- Now tell children that the area of the rectangle you are showing them is 24cm squared. Ask them what four different whole number lengths and widths could be? (1cm x 24cm, 2cm x 12cm, 3cm x 8cm, 4cm x 6cm.)
- Challenge children to think of decimal number possibilities that would give an area of 24cm squared. For example, 2.5cm x 9.6cm. Give out calculators for children to use.
- Discuss ways of working out how to find decimal number possibilities using a calculator. For example, 24cm divided by 9.6cm makes 2.5cm, so 2.5cm x 9.6cm = 24cm squared.
- Draw the rectangles you have calculated.

Variations

- Can you draw six different rectangles each with an area of 18 square cm?
- Why not investigate the different possibilities for other shapes too. For example, can you draw two different triangles with an area of 10cm squared?

Challenge questions

- Can you draw two congruent rectangles with a total area of 24 square cm?
- 24 divided by a 6.6 gives 3.6363636 so why is it that 6.6 x 3.6363636 doesn't make 24?
- Is it possible to reduce the perimeter of a shape and yet increase its area? Can you draw two different rectangles each with a perimeter of 24cm?

Happy numbers

Happy numbers is an activity that has a variety of mathematical uses and makes an excellent investigational mini-project.

Suitable for

KS2

Aims

- To square and add numbers.
- To find the digital root of numbers.
- To spot patterns and number cycles.

Players

- Pairs, small group, whole-class

Resources

- Paper and pencils (or whiteboards and pens)

What to do

- Tell children that some numbers are happy and some unhappy.
- Explain why 23 is a happy number.

  23 can be separated into 2 and 3
  2 squared is 4 and 3 squared is 9
  $4 + 9 = 13$
  13 can be separated into 1 and 3
  1 squared is 1 and 3 squared is 9
  $1 + 9 = 10$
  10 can be separated into 1 and 0
  1 squared is 1 and 0 squared is 0

1 + 0 is 1 so 23 is a happy number because it can be reduced to 1 through this process of squaring and adding.

- Now let children investigate the first 50 numbers. How many of these are happy?
- Discuss whether there is a quick way of telling whether a number is happy or not.

Variations

- Work out whether 3-digit numbers are happy or not.
- Find out whether your age, weight and height are happy numbers.
- Work out which happy numbers are also happy primes.

Challenge questions

- What if a number never comes to 1? How will you know? At what point do you know a number is unhappy?
- Are there an infinite number of happy numbers?
- Can you find a pattern in the sequence of happy numbers you have found?

Magic threes

Magic threes is a fantastic activity to get children thinking about how to combine four threes and any mathematical operation to make the numbers from 1 to 15.

Suitable for

KS2

Aims

- To creatively combine number operations.
- To work flexibly with a range of numbers.

Players

- Pairs, small group, whole-class

Resources

- Paper and pencils (or whiteboards and pens)

What to do

- Explain to children that the number 1 can be made using four 3s. Demonstrate how this can be done. For example, $3 \div 3 = 1$ added to $3 \div 3$ is 1, then 1 divided by 1 is 1. Can they think of another way of making one using four 3s? There is normally more than one way.
- Now challenge children to think together in small groups how they might make the number 2. Take answers after a period of working out and share ideas.
- Now challenge children to find all the numbers up to 15 using four 3s using addition, subtraction, multiplication, division, square roots and brackets.

Variations

- If children find all the numbers up to 15, increase the level of challenge up to 25.
- Play the same investigation game with other numbers. For example, try to make the numbers from 1 to 15 using four 4s or four 5s.

Challenge questions

- Is it possible to make 100 using four 3s?
- What are the smallest and largest numbers that can be made using four 3s?
- How far can you go with four 3s?

Number hop

> Number hop is a great game for mental number work helping children to practise multiplication, division, addition and subtraction.

Suitable for

KS1
KS2

Aims

- To creatively combine number operations.
- To work flexibly with a range of numbers.

Players

- Pairs, small group, whole-class

Resources

- Paper and pencils (or whiteboards and pens)
- Number cards 1–9

What to do

- Shuffle the cards and select two cards to make a 2-digit number.
- Challenge children to change the 2-digit number created into 10 in just two number/operation hops.
- For example, if 4 and 5 are selected to make 45, then 45 can be reduced to 10 by dividing by 5 and then adding one. Can children find other ways to get to 10? Investigate together ($\div 9$ and x2, $\div 9$ and +5, x2 and $\div 9$, –5 and $\div 4$, +5 and $\div 5$).
- Play the game as a whole class first to familiarise children with it and then let children play in small groups or in pairs.
- Challenge children to work out whether all 2-digit numbers can be reduced to 10 in two hops.

Variations

- Rather than make 10 in two hops, change to 'three' hops.
- Rather than deal two cards, deal three cards and reduce to a new number.

Challenge questions

- Which 2-digit numbers have the most ways of making 10?
- Is there a connection between the number of possibilities and number of factors?
- Do numbers in a particular times table have more possibilities?

Spot on

> Spot on is a number target game ideal for mental and written manipulation of the four operations. The game encourages mental agility, perseverance and speed of working.

Suitable for

KS1
KS2

Aims

- To combine number operations in order to make a target number.
- To work flexibly with a range of numbers.

Players

- This game can be played individually, in pairs or in a small group

Resources

- Paper and pencils (or whiteboards and pens)
- Four sets of number cards 1–10

What to do

- Shuffle the cards. Now select two cards from the pile. This is the target number.
- Deal each player five cards.
- Explain that the aim of the game is to make the target number using all five cards and any of the number operations. Numbers can be used once only unless they appear more than once in the cards dealt. Number operations can be used more than once.

- The first player to make the target number with their cards then shows everyone else their working out. If the working out is correct then the target number of points is scored.
- Shuffle the cards again and repeat the game by choosing two new cards to make another target number.
- After an agreed number of hands or after a certain time limit, the winner is the player with the most points.

Variations

- This game could be played with playing cards.
- The target number could be selected by randomly opening a book at a particular page number.
- Deal more or less cards as appropriate.

Challenge questions

- What other ways can you think of for choosing the target number?
- Are there target numbers that are more difficult to make?
- Is there an impossible target number to make?

Countdown

Countdown is based on the numbers game of the television show *Countdown*. This game tests children's mental agility in making a target number using any of the four operations.

Suitable for

KS1
KS2

Aims

- To combine number operations in order to make a target number.
- To work flexibly with a range of numbers.

Players

- This game can be played individually, in pairs or in a small group

Resources

- Paper and pencils (or whiteboards and pens)
- A set of 'high' number cards (25, 50, 75, 100) and 20 digit cards 1–9
- Die labelled 4–9

What to do

- Explain to children how the game of Countdown works. Show them a clip from the show if possible showing the numbers game. Explain that the aim is to get as close as possible to a randomly selected 3-digit number.
- Explain that in the game contestants select any 6 cards. Usually one or two of these are selected from a set of 4 high cards: 25, 50, 75 and 100. The other 5 or 4 cards are normally picked from twenty 1-9 digit cards. Any operation is allowed.

- Tell children that they don't have to use all six cards.
- Now have someone select six cards for the class to use, e.g. 25, 50, 2, 6, 3, 4.
- Roll a die three times to make a 3-digit number, e.g. 548.
- Set a time limit of one minute or longer for children to make the target number.
- Anyone who makes the target number scores the target number itself.
- Anyone who makes a number within 10 of the target number scores half the target number.
- Agree on a set number of rounds after which the player with the most points is the winner.

Variations

- If children struggle to make a number then they can turn over up to three more cards at a penalty of 50 points per card.
- Play the game where all six cards have to be combined to make the target number.
- Play the game with three high numbers and four low numbers.
- Set a stricter time limit.
- Make the target number a 4-digit number.

Challenge questions

- Can you think of a different scoring system? For example, use only five cards and score an extra 75 points.
- How can the game be made more challenging? For example, what about using decimal numbers?
- Can you devise a target game to practise fractions?

What's my house number?

What's my house number? involves children in thinking about numbers and formulating questions about them.

Suitable for

KS1
KS2

Aims

- To develop confidence recognising numbers and their properties.
- To ask appropriate questions relating to a range of numbers.

Players

- A whole-class game organised into four main groups

Resources

- Paper and pencil

What to do

- Divide the class into four teams and give each team a name, e.g. red, blue, green, yellow.
- Two teams play against each other while the other two teams watch and listen.
- The red team choose a number and write it on a piece of paper which is then folded and handed to the teacher. The number to be selected is less than 100.
- Members of the blue team then take it in turns to ask questions about the number, for example:

  Is the number less than 60? **Yes**
  Is it an odd number? **Yes**

Will it divide exactly by 4? **No**
Will it divide exactly by 3? **No**
Will it divide exactly by 9? **Yes**
Is the number palindromic? **No**
Are the ten and unit digits both odd? **No**
Is it a prime number? **No**
Is it a square number? **Yes**
Is the number greater than 36? **Yes**
Is your house number 49? **Yes**

- Make a note of how many questions are asked before the mystery number is found.
- When the number has been found the other two teams play and the red and blue team listen to the sorts of questions they could possibly ask when it is their turn again.

Variations

- This game can be played by limiting the choice of numbers as being between 30 and 120.
- Play the game using decimals and fractions.

Challenge questions

- Are there any questions which help to narrow the field?
- What would make this a more challenging game?

Chessboard

Chessboard is an activity that encourages children to see shapes within shapes.

Suitable for

KS1
KS2

Aims

- To practise recognition of common everyday shapes.
- To solve shape problems.

Players

- An activity for small groups of three or four

Resources

- Grids showing different numbers of squares
- Chessboard

What to do

- Show children four small squares joined together and ask how many squares they can see.

- Did they spot four or five squares? If children didn't spot five squares, point out the four small squares and the larger square that acts as the perimeter square.

- Challenge children to find out the number of squares on a 3 x 3 board.
- How many squares are there on a 4 x 4 board?
- Now look at a 8 x 8 chessboard and challenge children to work out how many squares there are.
- Share discussions and solutions before revealing how many squares there are (there are actually 64 + 49 + 36 + 25 + 16 + 9 + 4 + 1 squares on a chessboard giving a total of 204).

Variations

- Look at rectangular boards and investigate how many squares there are. For example, how many squares can you see?

- Investigate other shapes such as triangles within triangles.

Challenge questions

- How many rectangles are there on an 8 x 8 chessboard?
- How many parallelograms are there on an 8 x 8 chessboard?

The gridlock problem

The gridlock problem is an activity that helps children search for patterns and work systematically searching for a solution.

Suitable for

KS1
KS2

Aims

- To suggest, plan and develop lines of enquiry.
- Represent and interpret sequences, patterns and relationships involving numbers and shapes.

Players

- An activity for small groups of three or four

Resources

- Grids showing different numbers of squares (4 x 4, 5 x 5, 6 x 6, 7 x 7, 8 x 8)
- Chessboard
- Coloured counters

What to do

- Show children a 4 x 4 grid or chessboard as follows:

- Tell children that their problem is to place four counters on the board so that nowhere are there two objects on the same row, column or diagonal.
- Give children some time to plan what to do and experiment moving the counters around the grid to find a solution.
- After 5–10 minutes share ideas and discuss solutions.
- Now set children the problem again using a 5 x 5 grid and 5 counters.

Variations

- Find a solution for a 6 x 6 grid using six counters.
- Find a solution for a 7 x 7 grid using seven counters.
- Find a solution for a 8 x 8 grid using eight counters.
- Play Gridlock 2. Show children the grid here, which has 24 spaces.

Give children 18 counters and challenge them to place an even number of counters in every row and every column.

Challenge questions

- Can you place five objects on a 4 x 4 grid?
- Can you solve each grid problem above in more than one way?
- Is there a solution that works for one grid that will work on another grid?

Balloon numbers

Balloon numbers challenges children to think hard about number properties and why, in a row of numbers, one may be the odd one out.

Suitable for

KS1
KS2

Aims

- To improve knowledge and understanding of number properties.
- To argue, reason and justify choices.

Players

- An activity for any number of participants

Resources

- Pencil and paper

What to do

- Tell children there are six numbers crowded in the basket of a hot air balloon which is quickly losing height.
- To save the balloon from crashing, children in 2s or 3s have to decide which number should be ejected, and more importantly, *why* that number should leave.
- Provide some examples to get children started.
- For example, imagine the numbers in the basket are 5, 10, 15, 20, 25 and 30. You could argue that 5 should go because it is the only single-digit number. Then again it could be 25 because that's the only square number. Number 30 has the most factors and so on.
- Hold a debate and discuss why certain numbers should be allowed to stay in the basket.

Variations

- Include decimal numbers and fractions instead of whole numbers.
- Place six shapes in the balloon basket instead and focus on shape properties, e.g. parallel lines, perpendicular lines, etc.

Challenge questions

- Were there any numbers that were harder to argue for?
- What else could you put in the balloon basket?

Number hunters

> Number hunters challenges children to hunt for particular types of number in their environment.

Suitable for

KS1
KS2

Aims

- To improve knowledge and understanding of number properties.

Players

- Children work in pairs or small groups

Resources

- Pencil and paper

What to do

- Organise children into pairs or small groups of three or four.
- Tell children that they are going to go on a number quest looking for types of number. To start with, challenge them to find 12 prime numbers in the classroom.
- Children keep a list of the numbers they find and what the numbers relate to. For example, 2nd – today's date, 13 – the number of girls in the class, 7 – classroom number, etc.
- The rule is that no more than two numbers can come from the same place. For example, you cannot just take numbers from a book. The primes have to come from different sources.
- After five or ten minutes, talk together as a class and share the primes found.
- Now start a new number hunt and look for composite numbers.

Variations

- Look for primes and composites around the school.
- Children can find at least 12 of each type of number. Set a competition to find 30 for example.
- Search for other numbers, e.g. square, triangular, rectangular, cube, etc.

Challenge questions

- Were particular types of number harder to find than others?
- What about invisible numbers? For example, the weight of something, the length of an object, etc.
- Could you do the same for shapes?

Numbers are odd things

Numbers are odd things challenges children to investigate what happens when combinations of odd and even numbers are added together.

Suitable for

KS1
KS2

Aims

- To plan and pursue an enquiry.
- Present evidence by collecting, organising and interpreting data.
- Explore patterns, properties and relationships.

Players

- This is an activity suitable for maths buddies or small groups

Resources

- Pencil and paper

What to do

- Ask children to choose any two odd numbers and add them together. What do they notice?
- Do this again, many times. What do they notice?
- What happens when three odd numbers are added together?
- What happens if two even numbers are added together?
- What happens if an odd number and an even number are added together? Is there a pattern?
- Challenge children to draw up a table of odd and even rules for adding.

Variations

- Investigate what happens when you subtract odd and even numbers.
- Investigate what happens when you multiply odd and even numbers.
- Draw up a table of odd and even rules for adding, subtracting and multiplying.

Challenge questions

There are many challenge scenarios to follow. For example:
- Why do two odd numbers equal an even number but two even numbers won't equal an odd?
- Can you find two even numbers whose sum is not an even number? Why not?
- How can you tell that 6 and 8 are even numbers?
- What happens when you add five odd numbers and one even number?
- What is the result of multiplying an odd number with an odd number?
- What do you notice when you add two consecutive odd numbers?
- What happens when an odd number is subtracted from an even number? What about subtracting an odd number from an odd number?
- Jagdeep added 216 and 3348 and made 3545. Without adding how can you be sure that his addition is incorrect based on the odd and even rules you have learned?

Reach for one

Reach for one is an interesting and challenging investigation that focuses on an unusual sequence using simple numbers.

Suitable for

KS1
KS2

Aims

- To plan and pursue an enquiry.
- Present evidence by collecting, organising and interpreting data.
- Explore patterns, properties and relationships.

Players

- This is an activity suitable for maths buddies or small groups

Resources

- Pencil and paper
- Calculators

What to do

- Ask children to select a whole number.
- If an odd number is chosen then multiply by 3 and then add 1.
- If an even number is chosen, divide by 2.
- Take the result in 2 or 3 above and repeat.
- Continue to do this until you reach 1.
- Ask children to try the following numbers: 6, 10, 12, 40, 52.

Variations

- Ask children to copy and complete a table of numbers of your own choosing, e.g.

Number	3	5	12	14	17	23	32	35	39	42	45
Number of steps to reach 1											

- Investigate what happens if you change the rules for the sequence. For example, if the number is odd, multiply by 3 and subtract 1. If the number is even, divide by 2.

Challenge questions

- Can you find a number that does not produce a final result of 1?
- Which 2-digit number takes the most steps to reach 1?
- Which 3-digit number takes the most steps to reach 1?

Chapter 10
Brain-teasers

Up and down

Up and down is a very thought-provoking investigation that challenges children to use a variety of problem-solving skills.

Suitable for

KS2

Aims

- Describe ways of solving puzzles and problems, explaining choices and decisions orally or using pictures.
- Explain reasoning using diagrams, graphs and text.
- To plan and pursue an enquiry.
- Explore patterns, properties and relationships.

Players

- This is an activity suitable for maths buddies or small groups

Resources

- Pencil and paper
- Calculators

What to do

- Introduce children to the problem in the style of a short story as follows: a snail crawls 4m up a wall during the daytime. After all the effort of climbing the snail stops for a while to rest and then falls asleep. The next morning the snail wakes up to find it has slipped down 1m while asleep.
- Now set children the challenge itself: if this happens every day, how many days will the snail take to reach the top of a wall 58m in height?

- Allow children to reflect on the problem independently before organising children into pairs or small groups.
- Listen to children's ideas and the strategies they would use to solve the problem. How different are they?
- Now let children work together in mixed ability pairs/groups to solve the problem.
- Remind children of the UPR problem-solving process they need to take when approaching a problem such as this. For example,

  Understanding the problem (What do you need to know? What do you need to find out?)
  Planning and communicating a solution (How will you solve the problem?)
  Reflecting and generalising (Can more than one strategy be used?)

- You may want to provide children with a planning sheet in order to solve the problem or let them invent their own.
- Share ideas together and talk through the problem.
- Describe that one way of solving this problem would be to draw a diagram which you could model or get a pair/group to model.
- Now explain the solution as follows:

  On the first day, the snail climbs up 4m and slips down 1m while sleeping. This means the next morning the snail is 3m from where it started. The snail thus travels 3m upwards every day. Therefore, in 18 days, it has travelled a distance of 54m from the bottom. On the last day, the snail travels 4m upwards and hence reaches the top of the wall in a total of 19 days.

Variations

- This activity could be adapted for a spider trying to climb up a drainpipe. For example, a spider started climbing the side of a tall building. The building is 21m. It started climbing up the building at 6 a.m. It took the spider 15 minutes to climb 3m. At the end of every 15 minutes period the spider had a rest and slipped backwards 1m. What time did the spider reach the top of the building? If pupils draw a line to solve this problem they could show that the spider would take 195 minutes to get to the top of the building and reach the top at 09.15 a.m.

Challenge questions

- Can you work out an alternative solution to this problem through an equation? For example, let x be the number of days the snail takes to reach the top of the wall 58m in height. On the last day, the snail will reach the top by travelling 4m upwards and there will not be any question of slipping down. The number of remaining days excluding the last day are $(x - 1)$. Since the snail climbs up 4m and slips down 1m while sleeping, it travels 3m upwards on each of these remaining days. So,

  Distance travelled on last day + distance travelled on remaining days = Wall height; or
  $4 + 3 (x - 1) = 58$

  On solving the above equation, we get

  $3 (x - 1) = 58 - 4 = 54$; or
  $x = (54 / 3) + 1 = 19$

Wheely good

Wheely good is a problem that encourages children to use visualisation skills in order to solve a problem.

Suitable for

KS2

Aims

- Describe ways of solving puzzles and problems, explaining choices and decisions orally or using pictures.
- Explain reasoning using diagrams, graphs and text.
- To plan and pursue an enquiry.
- Explore patterns, properties and relationships.

Players

- This is an activity suitable for maths buddies or small groups

Resources

- Pencil and paper
- Calculators

What to do

- Introduce the problem to children as a story as follows:

  Last weekend, Jasmin went to play in the park on her new bike she received for her birthday. When she got to the park, she saw that there were a total of 19 bicycles and tricycles. If the total number of wheels was 47, how many tricycles were there?

- Repeat the question again and set children off in pairs to solve the problem using whatever strategies they deem appropriate.

- After a period of thinking and talking together, share ideas so far and ask for volunteers to demonstrate their strategy.
- Talk through as many ways of solving the problem with children before explaining the solution as follows.
- 19 bicycles will have 38 wheels so $47 - 38 = 9$ extra wheels. As bicycles have 2 wheels and tricycles have 3 wheels, there is 1 extra wheel per tricycle in the park. Thus, the 9 extra wheels belong to 3 tricycles.
- Check children's understanding of the problem and ask for someone to explain the solution to the class.

Variations

- This problem could be adapted for any number of wheels.
- Include Jasmin's bike in the problem (make it either a bicycle or a tricycle).
- What about including a unicycle in the problem?

Challenge questions

- Can you draw the solution to your problem?
- Can you use a problem-solving plan to work through this solution?
- A bike shop sells bicycles and tricycles. If there are 25 wheels in the shop, how many are bicycles and how many are tricycles?

Solution: there are 11 bicycles and 1 tricycle in the shop.

Bicycles	1	2	3	(+1 each time)	11
Tricycles	11	10	9	(−1 each time)	1
Wheels	35	34	33	(−1 each time)	25

A sticky problem

A sticky problem is an interesting challenge that encourages children to act out the problem or use a drawing.

Suitable for

KS2

Aims

- Describe ways of solving puzzles and problems, explaining choices and decisions orally or using pictures.
- Explain reasoning using diagrams, graphs and text.
- To plan and pursue an enquiry.
- Explore patterns, properties and relationships.

Players

- This is an activity suitable for maths buddies or small groups

Resources

- Pencil and paper
- Art straw

What to do

- Introduce the problem to the class:

  A witch retires from her job and decides to saw her broomstick into eight pieces for firewood. Each cut takes her 20 seconds. How long will it take her to cut the broomstick into pieces?

- Give the problem to pairs of children for a 2-minute discussion before taking feedback from the class as a whole. Talk about different ways of potentially solving the problem. Is there a strategy that would be more efficient than another?
- Now give each pair some art straws and scissors as something they could use to help them solve the problem.

- Remind the children of the UPR problem-solving approach to the challenge:

  Understanding the problem (What do you need to know? What do you need to find out?)
  Planning and communicating a solution (How will you solve the problem?)
  Reflecting and generalising (Can more than one strategy be used?)

- Probably the most common mistake in this problem is understanding how many cuts the witch will make. Many children will say that the witch will make eight cuts as she wants eight pieces. If they answer in this way then they will work out 8 x 20 seconds = 160 seconds or 2 minutes and 40 seconds.
- Take children's answers and talk through them together. Do the children realise that the witch will only need to make 7 cuts, which is 7 x 2 = 140 seconds or 2 minutes and 20 seconds?
- Show this as a drawing on the board and demonstrate using art straws.

Variations

- Instead of art straws you could use plasticine, strips of paper or string.
- This problem lends itself to many adaptations. For example, the number of cuts could be changed to a bigger or smaller number. The time taken to make a cut could also be changed. For example, a workman is cutting a metal pipe into 9 pieces. It takes him 16 seconds to make one cut. How long will it take him to cut the pipe into 9 pieces?

Challenge questions

- Did you realise that the end pieces are not cut?
- Why is it a good idea to use more than one strategy when solving a problem like this?
- Can you invent a problem similar to the one above but have each cut taking 10.25 seconds? Does this make it more challenging?

Two is company and 'tree' is a crowd

Two is company and 'tree' is a crowd is a seemingly easy challenge that requires a trial-and-error approach to solving the problem using a diagram.

Suitable for

KS2

Aims

- Describe ways of solving puzzles and problems, explaining choices and decisions orally or using pictures.
- Explain reasoning using diagrams, graphs and text.
- To plan and pursue an enquiry.
- Explore patterns, properties and relationships.

Players

- This is an activity suitable for maths buddies or small groups

Resources

- Pencil and paper
- 5 x 5 square grids

What to do

- Introduce the problem to children as follows:

  Morgan decides to plant 10 trees in a part of the school grounds. To help her the caretaker has painted a 5 x 5 square grid on a part of the school field. Morgan wants to plant the trees in such as way that no more than two trees lie in a line in any direction. Can you help her?

- Now give children a sheet of 5 by 5 square grids to help them work out an answer as follows:

- Ask children how they might solve the problem. What ideas do they have?
- Look at the grid completed by a fictitious pupil below. What do they think of the way the grid has been completed?

X		X		
	X		X	
		X		X
X			X	
	X			X

- Give children some talking and working time in order to solve the problem together.
- After a period of working, share possible solutions and share the following answer with children:

X		X		
X			X	
	X		X	
	X			X
		X		X

Variations

- The grid size could be increased.
- The number of trees could be increased.

Challenge questions

- Can you solve the problem in fewer than three tries?
- How many different solutions can you find?
- Does rotating the grid qualify as finding more than one solution?

Bookworms

Bookworms is a great challenge that requires children to adopt a systematic approach to solving a problem by drawing a table.

Suitable for

KS2

Aims

- Describe ways of solving puzzles and problems, explaining choices and decisions orally or using pictures.
- Explain reasoning using diagrams, graphs and text.
- To plan and pursue an enquiry.
- Explore patterns, properties and relationships.

Players

- This is an activity suitable for maths buddies or small groups

Resources

- Pencil and paper

What to do

- Introduce the problem to children as follows:

  Three Year 6 children decide to have a Bookworm reading competition. Every day Akemi reads five books, Brandon reads eight books and Aman reads three books. How many days will it take for the children to read a total of 96 books?

- Help children to understand the problem using a problem-solving step-by-step process.
- Ask children for ideas about how they might solve the problem.
- Talk through the problem and suggest drawing a table as an efficient strategy.

- Complete the table together so that children can see how to solve the problem logically. For example, talk through the completion of the table discussing any patterns as shown here.

Days	Akemi	Brandon	Aman	Total
1	5	8	3	16
2	10	16	6	32
3	15	24	9	48
4	20	32	12	64
5	25	40	15	80
6	30	48	18	96

- Compare and contrast any other methods children may have thought of.

Variations

- The number of books read by each pupil could be changed.
- Include more pupils when setting a different problem.

Challenge questions

- Can you invent a similar problem and include superfluous/redundant information for children to spot?
- Can you work out how many days it will take the children to read 208 books? (13)

Money bags

> Money bags is a trial-and-error challenge involving magic squares. This problem has many variations.

Suitable for

KS1
KS2

Aims

- Describe ways of solving puzzles and problems, explaining choices and decisions orally or using pictures.
- Explain reasoning using diagrams, graphs and text.
- To plan and pursue an enquiry.
- Explore patterns, properties and relationships.

Players

- This is an activity suitable for maths buddies or small groups

Resources

- Pencil and paper
- Magic square grids of different sizes, e.g. 3 x 3, 4 x 4, 5 x 5, etc.

What to do

- Introduce the problem to children as follows:

  You have nine bags of money containing the following amounts: £1, £2, £3, £4, £5, £6, £7, £8 and £9. You want to hide the bags in a 3 x 3 grid so that each row and column, whether horizontal, vertical or diagonal, has £15.

- Give children a 3 x 3 grid to work with and ask pairs to solve the problem in the quickest time. Is there more than one solution? Share one possible solution as follows:

£8	£1	£6
£3	£5	£7
£4	£9	£2

- Now ask children to find another solution, if they haven't already. For example,

£2	£7	£6
£9	£5	£1
£4	£3	£8

- What do they notice about the middle number?
- Now challenge children to fill a 4 x 4 grid with £1, £2, £3, £4, £5, £6, £7, £8, £9, £10, £11, £12, £13, £14, £15 and £16 so that each row, column and diagonal adds up to £34.
- Share with the children the solution shown here.

£16	£3	£2	£13
£5	£10	£11	£8
£9	£6	£7	£12
£4	£15	£14	£1

Variations

- You can make this harder by asking children to investigate a 5 x 5 magic square that adds up to 65. For example,

£3	£16	£9	£22	£15
£20	£8	£21	£14	£2
£7	£25	£13	£1	£19
£24	£12	£5	£18	£6
£11	£4	£17	£10	£23

Show children how to make a 4 x 4 magic square by following these instructions:

1. Enter any 16 consecutive numbers in a 4 x 4 grid as shown here.

5	6	7	8
9	10	11	12
13	14	15	16
17	18	19	20

2. Now switch the corner numbers along the diagonal.

20			17
8			5

3. Now switch the 4 centre numbers along the diagonal

20			17
	15	14	
	11	10	
8			5

4. Place the remaining numbers back in the square in their original positions

20	6	7	17
9	15	14	12
13	11	10	16
8	18	19	5

5. Add all the rows and columns and you will get 50 each time. For example,

20+6+7+17=50
9+15+14+12=50
13+11+10+16=50
8+18+19+5=50
20+9+13+8=50
6+15+11+18=50
7+14+10+19=50
20+15+10+5=50
8+11+14+17=50

Challenge questions

- Can you fill a 3 x 3 magic square using the first 9 consecutive even numbers: 2, 4, 6, 8, 10, 12, 14, 16, 18?
- How about the first 9 consecutive odd numbers: 1, 3, 5, 7, 9, 11, 13, 15, 17?
- Try to find another set of 9 different numbers that can form a 3 x 3 magic square.
- Can you construct a 3 x 3 magic square using any set of different numbers? See if you can prove it false by finding a counter-example: a set of 9 different numbers that cannot form a magic square.
- Can you prove that a 2 x 2 magic square is impossible?

How much?

> How much? is a challenge that encourages children to use a guess and checking method to solve the problem.

Suitable for

KS2

Aims

- Describe ways of solving puzzles and problems, explaining choices and decisions orally or using pictures.
- Explain reasoning using diagrams, graphs and text.
- To plan and pursue an enquiry.
- Explore patterns, properties and relationships.

Players

- This is an activity suitable for maths buddies

Resources

- Pencil and paper

What to do

- Introduce the problem to children as follows:

  Aisha went to the cinema with her friends. She bought some popcorn and a drink for £2.85. The popcorn cost twice as much as the drink. Can you work out the cost of each one?

- Before organising children into pairs, give children time to think independently about what they would do to solve the problem.
- Children get into pairs and then decide what strategy to follow.
- You could present some answers to children from fictitious children and the solutions they came up with. For example, Sohail and Iman think that the drink cost £0.95 and the popcorn cost £1.70.

- Share ideas with children and share the strategies children have.
- Go through the solution using a 'guess and check' strategy.
- Explain to children that drawing a table is a good way of starting the problem-solving process. For example,

	Drink	Popcorn	Total	Low/high/exact
Guess 1	£0.75	£1.50	£2.25	Too low
Guess 2	£1.00	£2.00	£3.00	Too high
Guess 3	£0.80	£1.60	£2.40	Too low
Guess 4	£0.95	£1.90	£2.85	Exact

Variations

- You can alter the amounts paid for the popcorn and drink accordingly.
- You could change the things being bought and the scenario.
- You could use plastic coins to experiment with the amounts.

Challenge questions

- Can you invent your own version of this problem involving two or three people and what they bought?
- How can this question be extended?
- How difficult would this problem be to solve without using a table?
- Could you invent a similar problem using a different currency?

999

999 is an open-ended number problem that challenges children to make the number 999 using nine digits.

Suitable for

KS2

Aims

- Describe ways of solving puzzles and problems, explaining choices and decisions orally or using pictures.
- Explain reasoning using diagrams, graphs and text.
- To plan and pursue an enquiry.
- Explore patterns, properties and relationships.

Players

- This is an activity suitable for maths buddies

Resources

- Pencil and paper

What to do

- Write the numbers from 1 to 9 on the whiteboard and ask children to choose one of them and tell the class three things about that number. For example, number 2, it is an even number, it is a prime number and it has two factors, 1 and 2.
- Now ask the children to think about combining numbers together. Explain that two 3-digit numbers have to be added together in order to make a total of 999. Which pair can find a solution first?
- After the first pair have shared their two 3-digit numbers, challenge children to find as many other possible combinations of numbers that give a total of 999.

- For example, some solutions are as follows:

  123
  + 876
  ─────
  999

  234
  + 765
  ─────
  999

  537
  + 462
  ─────
  999

Variations

- You could try playing this game to make 99 using two 2-digit numbers.
- Find the digital root of each row of numbers – do you notice anything?
- You could try this investigation by including numbers 0–9 rather than 1–9. Does this make a difference?

Challenge questions

- How many solutions do not include the digit 1?
- How many solutions do not include the digit 5?
- How many solutions do not contain the digit 8?
- Is it possible to use just odd numbers to make 999?

Ice cream

Ice cream is a problem that requires children to look for a pattern in order to solve the problem.

Suitable for

KS2

Aims

- Describe ways of solving puzzles and problems, explaining choices and decisions orally or using pictures.
- Explain reasoning using diagrams, graphs and text.
- To plan and pursue an enquiry.
- Explore patterns, properties and relationships.

Players

- This is an activity suitable for maths buddies

Resources

- Pencil and paper

What to do

- Introduce the problem to children as follows:

  At the beginning of July, a shop sells 1 bottle of water on the first day. The weather gradually gets warmer and it sells 2 on the second, 4 on the third, and 8 on the fourth. How many bottles of water is the shop likely to sell on the 11th day if the weather continues to improve?

- Reread the problem to children and make sure they understand what it is they have to do.
- Share ways of solving the problem as a whole class.

- Give pairs of children time to discuss and solve the problem together using the strategy they think will be the most useful.
- Encourage children to think about finding a pattern.
- Help children get started if they are struggling by drawing a table on the board.
- Share the solution with children using the table shown here.

Day	Water bottles
1	1
2	2
3	4
4	8
5	16
6	32
7	64
8	128
9	256
10	512
11	1,024
12	2,048

Variations

- This problem could be adapted by changing the starting number. For example, on day one the shop sold 3 bottles, on day two it sold 6 bottles, on the third day it sold 12 bottles, etc. Can you find how many bottles were sold by the 9th day?
- Change bottles of water to pages read day by day over the summer holiday.

Challenge questions

- Using the problem above, if 2,048 bottles were sold on the 12th day, does this mean that 4,096 bottles were sold on the 24th day?
- Can you double numbers starting at 4 up to the 20th number in your head?

Bonjour

Bonjour is a problem that requires children to create an organised list in order to reach a solution.

Suitable for

KS2

Aims

- Describe ways of solving puzzles and problems, explaining choices and decisions orally or using pictures.
- Explain reasoning using diagrams, graphs and text.
- To plan and pursue an enquiry.
- Explore patterns, properties and relationships.

Players

- This is an activity suitable for maths buddies.

Resources

- Pencil and paper
- Calculators

What to do

- Tell children that 25 French people met for a class reunion. Can they work out how many 'Bonjour's were said if no one said 'Bonjour' to anyone else who had already said 'Bonjour' to them?
- This problem may lend itself to acting out a solution if you have 25 in class.
- Discuss an alternative strategy if acting out isn't practical. What else could you do?

- Talk through the problem with children by creating an organised list. For example,

  The 1st guest says 24 Bonjours (one Bonjour to everyone at the reunion)
  The 2nd guest says 23 Bonjours (because the 1st person has already said Bonjour to them)
  The 3rd guest says 22 Bonjours
  The 4th guest says 21 Bonjours
  The 5th guest says 20 Bonjours, etc.

- Tell children that the easiest way to solve the problem is to add the numbers from 25–1 e.g. 25 + 24 + 23 + 22 + 21 + 20, etc. This results in 325 Bonjours in total.

Variations

- This scenario could be adapted for any number of people. For example, there are 65 guests at a party and each says 'Hello' to each other, etc.
- Try this problem for the number of handshakes at a party.

Challenge questions

- Can you find an easier way of adding the numbers 1–25? Which numbers would you add together to make it an easier sum to total?
- Can you invent a similar problem that involves 100 guests at a party? Is there a short cut way of finding the answer if you know how many Bonjours were said if 25 guests attended? Do you simply multiply by 4?

100 not out

> 100 not out is a brainteaser that encourages children to look for number combinations that make 100.

Suitable for

KS2

Aims

- Describe ways of solving puzzles and problems, explaining choices and decisions orally or using pictures.
- Explain reasoning using diagrams, graphs and text.
- To plan and pursue an enquiry.
- Explore patterns, properties and relationships.

Players

- This is an activity suitable for maths buddies

Resources

- Pencil and paper
- Calculators

What to do

- Write the following numbers on the board:

  32 39 34 27 33 29 31 35 28 40 38 41

- Now show children how three of those numbers can be joined together to make 100. For example, $32 + 33 + 35 = 100$.
- Now challenge children to find as many other combinations of three 2-digit numbers that they can which will make 100. Don't tell children how many combinations there are. See if they can find them – there are 12 more.

- Share combinations as a class and see how many they can find.
- Compare to the following:

27 + 32 + 41
27 + 34 + 39
27 + 35 + 38
27 + 33 + 40
28 + 31 + 41
28 + 32 + 40
28 + 33 + 39
28 + 34 + 38
29 + 32 + 39
29 + 33 + 38
29 + 31 + 40
31 + 34 + 35

Variations

- You could select different starting numbers and work out the combinations of those numbers which total to make 100.
- You could use 3-digit numbers as your starting numbers and challenge children to find number combinations to 1000.

Challenge questions

- Can you find any particular pattern to the numbers that make 100? For example, odd + even + odd. How many even + even + even = 100 combinations are there? How many odd + odd + odd = 100 combinations are there? How many mixed combinations are there?
- Have you noticed anything about the digital root of each number combination? Is it always the same?

Mystery number

Mystery number requires children to think hard about rows of numbers and the possible connections between them using addition and subtraction.

Suitable for

KS1
KS2

Aims

- Describe ways of solving puzzles and problems, explaining choices and decisions orally or using pictures.
- Explain reasoning using diagrams, graphs and text.
- To plan and pursue an enquiry.
- Explore patterns, properties and relationships.

Players

- This is an activity suitable for maths buddies

Resources

- Pencil and paper
- Calculators

What to do

- Write the following rows of numbers on the board or on a sheet of paper

$$3 \quad 4 \quad 5 \quad \mathbf{9} \quad 6 \quad 7 \quad 8$$
$$12 \quad 10 \quad 9 \quad \mathbf{10} \quad 11 \quad 16 \quad 14$$
$$7 \quad 3 \quad 2 \quad \mathbf{30} \quad 12 \quad 13 \quad 17$$
$$1 \quad 2 \quad 3 \quad \mathbf{24} \quad 9 \quad 10 \quad 11$$
$$51 \quad 7 \quad 8 \quad \mathbf{?} \quad 22 \quad 19 \quad 6$$

- Explain to children that there is a connection between the numbers on the right and left of the number in bold in each row. Can they work out what the ? stands for in the bottom row?
- Give children time to look at the rows and ask any questions.
- Remind children that there is a connection between the numbers and that they might have to use some number operations to help them, e.g. + − x ÷
- After a period of working see what sorts of answers children can suggest.
- If children are no closer to an answer then give them a clue, i.e. the two operations they need to solve the problem are + and −.
- Share one example with the children as follows: 3 + 4 + 5 = 12 and 6 + 7 + 8 = 21. If you subtract 21 and 12 you get 9. Can they see how it is done now?
- The middle number is the difference between the sums of the three numbers on the left and right. So, 51 + 7 + 8 = 66 and 22 + 19 + 6 = 47. This means that the ? is 66 − 47 which is 19.

Variations

- You can invent your own versions of these rows using smaller or larger numbers.
- Have just a couple of rows to start with.
- Play this as number columns instead.

Challenge questions

- Can you invent a version of this game using decimals or fractions?
- Can you invent a version of this game with more numbers on each row?
- Can you invent a version of this game using other number operations such as x and ÷?

Odd one out

Odd one out requires children to work out which row of numbers is the odd one out in a collection of rows.

Suitable for

KS1
KS2

Aims

- Describe ways of solving puzzles and problems, explaining choices and decisions orally or using pictures.
- Explain reasoning using diagrams, graphs and text.
- To plan and pursue an enquiry.
- Explore patterns, properties and relationships.

Players

- This is an activity suitable for maths buddies

Resources

- Pencil and paper

What to do

- Write the following number rows on the board or on a piece of paper:

```
A.  9  8  6  3  1  4  7
B.  6  1  5  3  2  0  3
C.  4  7  9  0  1  8  2
D.  1  6  7  2  1  0  4
E.  3  2  4  4  2  8  6
F.  4  6  7  3  1  1  2
G.  7  8  8  1  1  9  4
```

- Explain to children that there is an odd row in the collection of rows they can see and they have to work out which one it is and why.
- This problem could have many solutions because children will volunteer a variety of answers that could all feasibly be right. Explain that you will credit imaginative solutions but that you are really looking for just one solution.
- Give children some clues to help them solve the problem if you deem this appropriate. Explain that the middle three numbers are important in each row.
- Can the children see a link? If they can't, tell them to look at row A and total the middle 3 numbers (6 + 3 + 1 = 10). Now compare this to the middle three numbers of row B (5 + 3 + 2 = 10). This should be enough to set them racing off to find the middle digits which don't add up to 10.
- Row F is the odd row out because it contains three middle digits that total to 11.

Variations

- You can vary the numbers on either side and this will make little difference unless you alter the format so that the first number, middle number and last number always total, e.g. 15.
- Change the middle three numbers so that they total a new number, e.g. 14.
- Increase the number of digits in each row to complicate things further.

Challenge questions

- Can you invent a new format? For example, the 2nd number on the left and the 2nd to last always total 9.
- How many different reasons can you think of to justify one row being the odd one out compared to any other row?

Truth or lie

Truth or lie is an extended maths activity that requires children to be systematic in their approach to solving the problem.

Suitable for

KS1
KS2

Aims

- Describe ways of solving puzzles and problems, explaining choices and decisions orally or using pictures.
- Explain reasoning using diagrams, graphs and text.
- To plan and pursue an enquiry.
- Explore patterns, properties and relationships.

Players

- This is an activity suitable for maths buddies

Resources

- Pencil and paper

What to do

- Introduce the problem to children as follows:

  Kanezah was away from school for the school sports day. She asked six of her friends to tell her the number of the winner of a particular race. Only four of her friends gave the right answer. Using the clues below, which number was the winner?

Maimoona – it was even
Tehzeena – it was odd
Chloe – it was prime
Jake – it was a square number
Maisy – it had 2 digits
Megan – it was between 6 and 12

- Ask children to work in small groups or pairs to try and make sense of the problem together.
- Ask children to suggest ways of working out the solution. Check they understand the problem, i.e. it is the number they are looking for.
- Share with children a way of solving the problem if you find they are having difficulty.
- One of the best ways of solving the problem is to draw a table and work through a set of numbers systematically.
- Explain to children that this is a step-by-step problem that will reveal the result because 4 crosses in the table will mean 4 truths.

	Even	Odd	Prime	Square	Two digits	6-12
1		X		X		
2	X		X			
3		X	X			
4	X			X		
5		X	X			
6	X					X
7		X	X			X
8	X					X
9		X		X		X
10	X				X	X
11		**X**	**X**		**X**	**X**
12	X				X	X
13		X	X		X	
14	X				X	
15		X			X	
16	X			X	X	

- Using this method, you can see that the row with four crosses is row 11 so that means number 11 was the winner.

Variations

- You could add more children to the beginning or take some away.
- Have children say different things, e.g. it was a triangular number, it was a cube number, etc.

Challenge questions

- Can you work out which four friends were telling the truth?
- Can you invent another version of this activity with eight people?

What's next?

What's next? challenges children to be creative mathematicians solving a seemingly unrelated row of numbers.

Suitable for

KS1
KS2

Aims

- Describe ways of solving puzzles and problems, explaining choices and decisions orally or using pictures.
- Explain reasoning using diagrams, graphs and text.
- To plan and pursue an enquiry.
- Explore patterns, properties and relationships.

Players

- This is an activity suitable for maths buddies

Resources

- Pencil and paper

What to do

- Write the following numbers on the board

95	45	9	81	9
78	56	11	121	4
68	?	?	?	?

- Explain to children that the numbers in the first row are connected by some number operations so that one number leads to another. They have to work out which numbers will follow 68 in the third row.

- Give children time to look carefully at the first row and spot any connections.
- See what solutions children come up with before sharing the actual solution you are following.

Solution: Multiply the first two digits to make the 2nd number. Add the digits of the second number to get the 3rd number. Square the 3rd number to get the 4th number. Add the digits of the 4th number to get the last number. So, the missing numbers are:

68   48   12   144   9

Variations

- You can use a variety of operations or steps. For example, double the first number, find the digital root, multiply by 6 and then subtract 3.
- Try to solve the problem as a class by having children volunteer to write the numbers on a whiteboard and hold them in front of the whole class. This may help children to visualise the numbers and steps better.

Challenge question

- Can you invent your own number step problem like this, but arranging the numbers in a different way other than in a row? For example, you could have numbers on each vertex of a hexagon with a missing number in the middle.

Appendices

Thinking questions you could use

Can you explain in your own words what this problem is asking you to do?

What do you think the problem is asking?

Tell me about the problem. What do you know about the problem? Can you describe the problem to someone else?

Have you seen a problem like this before?

How accurate...?

How does...? How do...?

Are you able to...?

What must be added/removed/altered..?

Can you tell me what is wrong with...?

What maths do you think you will use in this game?

What is similar....? What is different...? What if...?

What needs to be changed so that...?

Is it or is it not...?

How can we be sure that...?

What would happen if...?

Is it always true that...?

Is it ever false that...?

Is it always, sometimes, never..?

Tell me something that must be true if...?

Which features of...make it an example of...?

Can you convince me that...?

I wonder whether...?

Suppose that we...?

Have you found all the solutions?

How do you know that...?

Why are...?

Why did...?

Where do...?

Can you prove that....?

Can you justify...?

Can you find a different method?

Could you have...?

How would we find...?

Can you add to that explanation?

What have you found out?

Do you think...?

Have you noticed that...?

What advice would you give someone else?

What was easy about this problem?

What was hard about this problem?

Would you expect...?

What exactly did you mean by...?

Why did you say...?

What were you thinking about when you said...?

Is there anything else you could say?

How does that compare with what you said before?

What would have to change in order for...?

What's another way you might...?

What would it look like if...?

How could you improve your argument?

What is the connection between...and...?

Do you need more evidence to...?

What else would you like to find out about this?

Is all the information you have gathered relevant?

What other information is needed in order to answer the question..?

Did you get the results you expected?

Can you describe, demonstrate, tell, show, choose, draw, find, locate, an example of...?

Is...an example of...?

Can you find a counter-example of...?

Give an example of a relationship between...and...

Are there any special examples of...?

What do you get if you change...to...?

Multiplication and division facts up to 10

$0 \times 1 = 0$
$1 \times 1 = 1$
$2 \times 1 = 2$
$3 \times 1 = 3$
$4 \times 1 = 4$
$5 \times 1 = 5$
$6 \times 1 = 6$
$7 \times 1 = 7$
$8 \times 1 = 8$
$9 \times 1 = 9$
$10 \times 1 = 10$

$0 \div 1 = 0$
$1 \div 1 = 1$
$2 \div 1 = 2$
$3 \div 1 = 3$
$4 \div 1 = 4$
$5 \div 1 = 5$
$6 \div 1 = 6$
$7 \div 1 = 7$
$8 \div 1 = 8$
$9 \div 1 = 9$
$10 \div 1 = 10$

$0 \times 2 = 0$
$1 \times 2 = 2$
$2 \times 2 = 4$
$3 \times 2 = 6$
$4 \times 2 = 8$
$5 \times 2 = 10$
$6 \times 2 = 12$
$7 \times 2 = 14$
$8 \times 2 = 16$
$9 \times 2 = 18$
$10 \times 2 = 20$

```
0 ÷ 2 = 0
2 ÷ 2 = 1
4 ÷ 2 = 2
6 ÷ 2 = 3
8 ÷ 2 = 4
10 ÷ 2 = 5
12 ÷ 2 = 6
14 ÷ 2 = 7
16 ÷ 2 = 8
18 ÷ 2 = 9
20 ÷ 2 = 10

0 x 3 = 0
1 x 3 = 3
2 x 3 = 6
3 x 3 = 9
4 x 3 = 12
5 x 3 = 15
6 x 3 = 18
7 x 3 = 21
8 x 3 = 24
9 x 3 = 27
10 x 3 = 30

0 ÷ 3 = 0
3 ÷ 3 = 1
6 ÷ 3 = 2
9 ÷ 3 = 3
12 ÷ 3 = 4
15 ÷ 3 = 5
18 ÷ 3 = 6
21 ÷ 3 = 7
24 ÷ 3 = 8
27 ÷ 3 = 9
30 ÷ 3 = 10
```

0 x 4 = 0
1 x 4 = 4
2 x 4 = 8
3 x 4 = 12
4 x 4 = 16
5 x 4 = 20
6 x 4 = 24
7 x 4 = 28
8 x 4 = 32
9 x 4 = 36
10 x 4 = 40

0 ÷ 4 = 0
4 ÷ 4 = 1
8 ÷ 4 = 2
12 ÷ 4 = 3
16 ÷ 4 = 4
20 ÷ 4 = 5
24 ÷ 4 = 6
28 ÷ 4 = 7
32 ÷ 4 = 8
36 ÷ 4 = 9
40 ÷ 4 = 10

0 x 5 = 0
1 x 5 = 5
2 x 5 = 10
3 x 5 = 15
4 x 5 = 20
5 x 5 = 25
6 x 5 = 30
7 x 5 = 35
8 x 5 = 40
9 x 5 = 45
10 x 5 = 50

$0 \div 5 = 0$
$5 \div 5 = 1$
$10 \div 5 = 2$
$15 \div 5 = 3$
$20 \div 5 = 4$
$25 \div 5 = 5$
$30 \div 5 = 6$
$35 \div 5 = 7$
$40 \div 5 = 8$
$35 \div 5 = 9$
$50 \div 5 = 10$

$0 \times 6 = 0$
$1 \times 6 = 6$
$2 \times 6 = 12$
$3 \times 6 = 18$
$4 \times 6 = 24$
$5 \times 6 = 30$
$6 \times 6 = 36$
$7 \times 6 = 42$
$8 \times 6 = 48$
$9 \times 6 = 54$
$10 \times 6 = 60$

$0 \div 6 = 0$
$6 \div 6 = 1$
$12 \div 6 = 2$
$18 \div 6 = 3$
$24 \div 6 = 4$
$30 \div 6 = 5$
$36 \div 6 = 6$
$42 \div 6 = 7$
$48 \div 6 = 8$
$54 \div 6 = 9$
$60 \div 6 = 10$

```
0 x 7 = 0
1 x 7 = 7
2 x 7 = 14
3 x 7 = 21
4 x 7 = 28
5 x 7 = 35
6 x 7 = 42
7 x 7 = 49
8 x 7 = 56
9 x 7 = 63
10 x 7 = 70

0 ÷ 7 = 0
7 ÷ 7 = 1
14 ÷ 7 = 2
21 ÷ 7 = 3
28 ÷ 7 = 4
35 ÷ 7 = 5
42 ÷ 7 = 6
49 ÷ 7 = 7
56 ÷ 7 = 8
63 ÷ 7 = 9
70 ÷ 7 = 10

0 x 8 = 0
1 x 8 = 8
2 x 8 = 16
3 x 8 = 24
4 x 8 = 32
5 x 8 = 40
6 x 8 = 48
7 x 8 = 56
8 x 8 = 64
9 x 8 = 72
10 x 8 = 80
```

$0 \div 8 = 0$
$8 \div 8 = 1$
$16 \div 8 = 2$
$24 \div 8 = 3$
$32 \div 8 = 4$
$40 \div 8 = 5$
$48 \div 8 = 6$
$56 \div 8 = 7$
$64 \div 8 = 8$
$72 \div 8 = 9$
$80 \div 8 = 10$

$0 \times 9 = 0$
$1 \times 9 = 9$
$2 \times 9 = 18$
$3 \times 9 = 27$
$4 \times 9 = 36$
$5 \times 9 = 45$
$6 \times 9 = 54$
$7 \times 9 = 63$
$8 \times 9 = 72$
$9 \times 9 = 81$
$10 \times 9 = 90$

$0 \div 9 = 0$
$9 \div 9 = 1$
$18 \div 9 = 2$
$27 \div 9 = 3$
$36 \div 9 = 4$
$45 \div 9 = 5$
$54 \div 9 = 6$
$63 \div 9 = 7$
$72 \div 9 = 8$
$81 \div 9 = 9$
$90 \div 9 = 10$

0 x 10 = 0
1 x 10 = 10
2 x 10 = 20
3 x 10 = 30
4 x 10 = 40
5 x 10 = 50
6 x 10 = 60
7 x 10 = 70
8 x 10 = 80
9 x 10 = 90
10 x 10 = 100

0 ÷ 10 = 0
10 ÷ 10 = 1
20 ÷ 10 = 2
30 ÷ 10 = 3
40 ÷ 10 = 4
50 ÷ 10 = 5
60 ÷ 10 = 6
70 ÷ 10 = 7
80 ÷ 10 = 8
90 ÷ 10 = 9
100 ÷ 10 = 10

Factors - all of the numbers 1-100

1: 1
2: 1, 2
3: 1, 3
4: 1, 2, 4
5: 1, 5
6: 1, 2, 3, 6
7: 1, 7
8: 1, 2, 4, 8
9: 1, 3, 9
10: 1, 2, 5, 10
11: 1, 11
12: 1, 2, 3, 4, 6, 12
13: 1, 13
14: 1, 2, 7, 14
15: 1, 3, 5, 15
16: 1, 2, 4, 8, 16
17: 1, 17
18: 1, 2, 3, 6, 9, 19
19: 1, 19
20: 1, 2, 4, 5, 10, 20
21: 1, 3, 7, 21
22: 1, 2, 11, 22
23: 1, 23
24: 1, 2, 3, 4, 6, 8, 12, 24
25: 1, 5, 25
26: 1, 2, 13, 26
27: 1, 3, 9, 27
28: 1, 2, 4, 7, 14, 28
29: 1, 29
30: 1, 2, 3, 5, 6, 10, 15, 30
31: 1, 31
32: 1, 2, 4, 8, 16, 32
33: 1, 3, 11, 33
34: 1, 2, 17, 34
35: 1, 5, 7, 35
36: 1, 2, 3, 4, 6, 9, 12, 18, 36
37: 1, 37

38: 1, 2, 19, 38
39: 1, 3, 13, 39
40: 1, 2, 4, 5, 8, 10, 20, 40
41: 1, 41
42: 1, 2, 3, 6, 7, 14, 21, 42
43: 1, 43
44: 1, 2, 4, 4, 11, 22, 44
45: 1, 3, 5, 9, 15, 45
46: 1, 2, 23, 46
47: 1, 47
48: 1, 2, 3, 4, 6, 8, 12, 16, 24, 48
49: 1, 7, 49
50: 1, 2, 5, 10, 25, 50
51: 1, 3, 17, 51
52: 1, 2, 4, 13, 26, 52
53: 1, 53
54: 1, 2, 3, 6, 9, 18, 27, 54
55: 1, 5, 11, 55
56: 1, 2, 4, 7, 8, 14, 28, 56
57: 1, 3, 19, 57
58: 1, 2, 29, 58
59: 1, 59
60: 1, 2, 3, 4, 5, 6, 10, 12, 15, 20, 30, 60
61: 1, 61
62: 1, 2, 31, 62
63: 1, 3, 7, 9, 21, 63
64: 1, 2, 4, 8, 16, 32, 64
65: 1, 5, 13, 65
66: 1, 2, 3, 6, 11, 22, 33, 66
67: 1, 67
68: 1, 2, 4, 17, 34, 68
69: 1, 3, 23, 69
70: 1, 2, 5, 7, 10, 14, 35, 70
71: 1, 71
72: 1, 2, 3, 4, 6, 8, 9, 12, 18, 24, 36, 72
73: 1, 73
74: 1, 2, 37, 74
75: 1, 3, 5, 15, 25, 75
76: 1, 2, 4, 19, 38, 76

77: 1, 7, 11, 77
78: 1, 2, 3, 6, 13, 26, 39, 78
79: 1, 79
80: 1, 2, 4, 5, 8, 10, 16, 20, 40, 80
81: 1, 3, 9, 27, 81
82: 1, 2, 41, 82
83: 1, 83
84: 1, 2, 3, 4, 6, 7, 12, 14, 21, 28, 42, 84
85: 1, 5, 17, 85
86: 1, 2, 43, 86
87: 1, 3, 29, 87
88: 1, 2, 4, 8, 11, 22, 44, 88
89: 1, 89
90: 1, 2, 3, 5, 6, 9, 10, 15, 18, 30, 45, 90
91: 1, 7, 13, 91
92: 1, 2, 4, 23, 46, 92
93: 1, 3, 31, 93
94: 1, 2, 47, 94
95: 1, 5, 19, 95
96: 1, 2, 3, 4, 6, 8, 12, 16, 24, 32, 48, 96
97: 1, 97
98: 1, 2, 7, 14, 49, 98
99: 1, 3, 9, 11, 33, 99
100: 1, 2, 4, 5, 10, 20, 25, 50, 100

Prime numbers less than 100

Prime numbers less than 100

Primes less than 20	2, 3, 5, 7, 11, 13, 17, 19
Primes between 20 and 40	23, 29, 31, 37
Primes between 40 and 60	41, 43, 47, 53, 59
Primes between 60 and 80	61, 67, 71, 73, 79
Primes between 80 and 100	83, 89, 97

Composite numbers less than 100

4, 6, 8, 9, 10, 12, 14, 15, 16, 18, 20, 21, 22, 24, 25, 26, 27, 28, 30, 32, 33, 34, 35, 36, 38, 39, 40, 42, 44, 45, 46, 48, 49, 50, 51, 52, 54, 55, 56, 57, 58, 60, 62, 63, 64, 65, 66, 68, 69, 70, 72, 74, 75, 76, 77, 78, 80, 81, 82, 84, 85, 86, 87, 88, 90, 91, 92, 93, 94, 95, 96, 98, 99.

Square numbers 1-20

1 x 1 = 1
2 x 2 = 4
3 x 3 = 9
4 x 4 = 16
5 x 5 = 25
6 x 6 = 36
7 x 7 = 49
8 x 8 = 64
9 x 9 = 81
10 x 10 = 100
11 x 11 = 121
12 x 12 = 144
13 x 13 = 169
14 x 14 = 196
15 x 15 = 225
16 x 16 = 256
17 x 17 = 289
18 x 18 = 324
19 x 19 = 361
20 x 20 = 400

The four-step problem-solving process

Step 1: Understanding the problem

What do we know?
What do we need to find out?

Step 2: Decide on a strategy

What strategies could we use to solve this problem?
Can we solve the problem in more than one way?
Which strategy is the most efficient?

Acting it out?
Working backwards?
Using logical reasoning?
Drawing a table?
Drawing a diagram?
Guess and check?
Looking for a pattern?
Creating a list?
Analysing and investigating?

Step 3: Solving the problem

How will we record our ideas and steps?
How can we be systematic?
How can we double-check our ideas?

Step 4: Reflect, revise, refine

What could we have done differently?
What if we had a similar problem to solve?

Glossary

Some useful key concepts..

Add to add things, you join or connect them to each other
Adjacent adjoining (as used to describe lines and angles)
Alternate every other one in a sequence
Ascending order the arrangement of numbers from smallest to largest
Average a number representing a set of numbers (obtained by dividing the total of the numbers by the numbers itself)

Baker's dozen the name given to the number 13
Base the line or face on which a shape is standing
Billion a thousand million, e.g. 1,000,000,000 (US definition).
Billion a million million, eg. 1,000,000,000,000 (UK definition).
Bisect to divide into two equal parts
Breadth breadth is another name for width. It is the distance across from side to side.

Cardinal number a number that shows quantity but not order
Carroll diagram a problem-solving diagram used in classification activities
Composite number a number with more than two factors
Congruent congruent shapes are the same shape and size (equal)
Consecutive consecutive numbers follow in order without interruption (e.g. 2,3,4,5)
Coordinates numbers used to locate a point on a grid

Denominator the number below the line in a fraction
Descending order the arrangement of numbers from largest to smallest
Diagonal a straight line connecting two non-adjacent vertices (corners) of a polygon
Difference the amount by which a number is bigger or smaller than another
Digit any number from 0 to 9 (inclusive)
Digital root the digital root of 38 is 2 because $3 + 8 = 11$ and $1 + 1 = 2$
Dodecagon a twelve-sided polygon

Edge the intersection of two faces of a three-dimensional object
Equation a statement of equality between two expressions (e.g. $3 \times 4 = 6 + 6$)

Even number a positive or negative number exactly divisible by 2
Exterior outside

Face a plane surface of a three-dimensional object
Face value the numeral itself despite its position in a number (e.g. the face value of 7 in 379 is 7)
Factor a number which will divide exactly into another number

Greater than an inequality between numbers. The symbol used to represent greater than is an arrow pointing towards the smallest number (>)
Gross the name given to the number 144

Hendecagon a two-dimensional shape with eleven sides and eleven angles also called an undecagon
Heptagon a two-dimensional shape with seven sides and seven angles also called a septagon
Hexagon a polygon with six sides
Horizontal describes a line or plane parallel to the earth's surface

Improper fraction a fraction whose numerator is equal to or greater than its denominator
Integer a negative or positive whole number
Interior inside
Isosceles triangle a triangle which has two equal sides of equal length

Kilogram 1,000 grams
Kilolitre 1,000 litres

Less than an inequality between numbers. The symbol used to represent less than is an arrow pointing towards the largest number (<)

Mean the average of a set of numbers. The sum of the values in a set of data divided by the total number of items in that set
Median the middle value of a set of ordered data
Mode the value that occurs the most often in a set of data
Multiple the product of a given number with another factor

Numerator the number above the line in a fraction.

Oblique means sloping or slanting.
Oblong a shape with two pairs of straight, unequal sides and four right angles. Also known as a rectangle.
Obtuse angle an angle between 90 and 180 degrees
Octagon a polygon with eight sides and eight angles
Odd number a number that when divided by two leaves a remainder of one
Ordinal number describes a position in a number sequence

Perimeter the length of the distance around the boundary of a shape
Perpendicular line a line at right angles to another line or plane
Place value indicates the position of a numeral (e.g. the place value of the 3 in 738 is 30)
Prime number a number with only two factors, 1 and itself (e.g. 2, 3, 5, 7, 11, 13, 17, 19, 23…)
Product the result when two or more numbers are multiplied

Quadrant a quarter of the area of a circle which also contains a right angle.
Quotient the result when one number is divided by another number.
Quindecagon a polygon with 15 sides and 15 angles.

Roman numerals seven letters are used in combination to write numbers:
I = 1
V = 5
X = 10
L = 50
C = 100
D = 500
M = 1000

Rounding an approximation used to express a number in a more convenient way

Score the name given to the number 20
Squared a number squared is a number multiplied by itself
Square number a number whose units can be arranged within a square (e.g. 1, 4, 9, 16, 25, 36, 49, 64…)
Sum the result when two or more numbers are added together
Symmetrical a shape is symmetrical if it is identical on either side of a line dividing it into two parts

Tally a record of items using vertical and oblique lines to represent each item
Triangular number a number whose units can be arranged within a triangle
(e.g. 1, 3, 6, 10, 15, 21...)

Vertex the point at which two or more line segments or two or more edges of a
polyhedron meet
Vertical line a line which is at right angles to a horizontal line

Classroom Gems

Innovative resources, inspiring creativity across the school curriculum

Designed with busy teachers in mind, the Classroom Gems series draws together an extensive selection of practical, tried-and-tested, off-the-shelf ideas, games and activities, guaranteed to transform any lesson or classroom in an instant.

Games and activities for
Primary Modern Foreign Languages
Teena Lomaster

© 2008 Paperback
ISBN: 9781405873925

Practical ideas, games and activities for the
Primary Classroom
Paul Barron

© 2008 Paperback
ISBN: 9781405859455

Games, ideas and activities for
Primary PE
Will Allen

© 2009 Paperback
ISBN: 9781408220382

Games, ideas and activities for
Learning Outside the Primary Classroom
Paul Barron

© 2009 Paperback
ISBN: 9781408225608

Games, ideas and activities for
Primary Literacy
Hazel Glynne and Amanda Snowden

© 2010 Paperback
ISBN: 9781408225516

Games, ideas and activities for
Primary Humanities
Richard Green

© 2009 Paperback
ISBN: 9781408228098

Games, ideas and activities for
Primary Music
Donna Minto

© 2009 Paperback
ISBN: 9781408223260

Games, ideas and activities for
Primary Drama
Michael Theodorou

© 2009 Paperback
ISBN: 9781408223291

Games, ideas and activities for
Early Years Phonics
Lynn Cousins and Gill Coulson

© 2009 Paperback
ISBN: 9781408224359

Creative activities for the
Secondary Classroom
Mark Labrow

© 2009 Paperback
ISBN: 9781408225578

Games, ideas and activities for
Primary Science
John Dabell

© 2010 Paperback
ISBN: 9781408223239

Longman
is an imprint of

PEARSON

'Easily navigable, allowing teachers to choose the right activity quickly and easily, these invaluable resources are guaranteed to save time and are a must-have tool to plan, prepare and deliver first-rate lessons'